Let's Talk Politics:

Restoring Civility Through Exploratory Discussion

SEPTEMBER 2014

SECOND EDITION

Let's Talk Politics

Adolf G. Gundersen, Ph.D.
Email: gundersen@interactivityfoundation.org

Suzanne Goodney Lea, Ph.D.
Email: lea@interactivityfoundation.org

The deliberative model of democracy has deep philosophical roots going back to Ancient Greece. Modern political science tests hypotheses about preconditions and consequences of good deliberation. Now is the time to put all this knowledge into everyday practice. Gundersen and Lea's book does this in an exemplary way. In a clear and jargon-free language, the authors show in great detail, how ordinary citizens can organize themselves into small discussion groups, where they can learn to listen to the arguments of others and to be open to the force of the better argument. The book reveals how successful the Interactivity Foundation already has been in engaging a large number of citizens in this important endeavor.

—**Jürg Steiner**, Professor of Political Science,
University of North Carolina at Chapel Hill,
The University of Bern (Switzerland), and
The European University Institute, Florence (Italy)

*In these uncivil times, how do we achieve democracy? How do ordinary people have a voice when the typical mode of politics is shouting at one another? In **Let's Talk Politics**, Gundersen and Lea provide an answer and a how-to guide for achieving it. In their vision, civil discussion with others is the political practice people need. This guide argues for Interactivity Foundation's discussions, in which groups of people talk about prepared public discussion reports on major public affairs issues in order to "sharpen their own truths." IF discussions may not attract the most cynical or the most partisan, but they very well may help foster a civic voice among the large swath of America who perceives no one is listening.*

—**Katherine Cramer**, Professor of Political Science
and Interim Director of the Morgridge Center for
Public Service, University of Wisconsin-Madison

In recent years, many democratic theorists have talked a great deal about the importance of thoughtful deliberation and civic discourse to healthy politics. The Interactivity Foundation does not merely talk about dialogue and civility but shows us ways to bring these ideals to life in the real world.

—**Thomas Spragens**, Professor of Political Science,
Duke University

Gundersen and Lea address the crucial problem of incivility that is plaguing contemporary societies. As they argue, a key part of the solution to increasing civility is participation in public discussion on policy issues. **Let's Talk Politics** *makes an important contribution to the increasing dominance of deliberative democracy. In particular, it focuses on the IF approach developed by the Interactivity Foundation and Jay Stern. Drawing on their experience running and researching a significant number of these citizen discussions, Gundersen and Lea provide evidence of the positive benefits these discussions have on various aspects of civility. Importantly, practical guidance is provided on how best to replicate these events. The book is therefore of interest to engaged citizens, practitioners, and academics alike. It focuses on America, but the guidance given on running similar policy discussion events to engage citizens is relevant to all countries, where they could have a similar impact on civility.*

—**Stephen Elstub**, Associate Professor of Politics,
University of the West of Scotland

This year marks the centennial of the birth of Jay Stern, originator of the process this book describes and founder of the Interactivity Foundation. We dedicate this book to him. We hope that its publication helps others keep the faith with his profound belief in the value of exploratory discussion.

Adolf G. Gundersen and Suzanne Goodney Lea

O sir, we quarrel in print, by the book; as you have books for good manners: I will name you the degrees. The first, the Retort Courteous; the second, the Quip Modest; the third, the Reply Churlish; the fourth, the Reproof Valiant; the fifth, the Countercheque Quarrelsome; the sixth, the Lie with Circumstance; the seventh, the Lie Direct. All these you may avoid but the Lie Direct; and you may avoid that too, with an If. I knew when seven justices could not take up a quarrel, but when the parties were met themselves, one of them thought but of an If, as, 'If you said so, then I said so;' and they shook hands and swore brothers. Your If is the only peacemaker; much virtue in If.

—William Shakespeare
(*As You Like It*, Act V, Scene IV)

Table of Contents

CHAPTER 1

— What's Wrong with Incivility?

We can never be sure that the opinion we are endeavoring to stifle is a false opinion; and if we were sure, stifling it would be an evil still.

~John Stuart Mill, *On Liberty*, 1859

On January 8, 2010, Congresswoman Gabrielle Giffords (D-AZ) and several of her constituents were shot in a Tucson, Arizona, parking lot while participating in an open-air town hall meeting. The shooter, a mentally ill young man, opened fire on the defenseless crowd, injuring 14 and killing six. The incident led the national media to proclaim that incivility was escalating in American society.

Of course, very few people resort to overt violence when faced with a congressional representative they feel doesn't represent their views. But nearly all of us know an uncle we think is "nuts" because he believes the election of President Barack Hussein Obama points to an Arab-orchestrated conspiracy against our nation, or a colleague who is absolutely convinced that food additives cause autism, or a holier-than-thou friend we'd just as soon un-friend. All of these folks can be dogmatic in their thinking and, as such, uncivil towards those who express opposing views.

Incivility may well be on the loose in American politics, but so what? Incivility is distasteful, sometimes disgusting, and occasionally downright offensive, but does it do real harm? We argue that it does indeed. Incivility does a great deal of harm to all of us as citizens and to what used to be called "the body politic" as well. It harms us individually and collectively. Even worse, these problems aren't just additive; they tend to reinforce one another. Incivility is like bullying: It hurts the victim and spreads the political equivalent of playground fear. As fear spreads, the bullies grow bolder and the victims more cowed.

Incivility isn't just ugly; it ultimately divides us into two camps: the loud and the silent. When this happens, the First Amendment's guarantees of free speech become ever more irrelevant. What is the point of free speech if all one can hear is shouting? And if no one is listening, what becomes of democracy—of what Abraham Lincoln, in his Gettysburg Address, called "rule of the people, by the people, and for the people"?

HOW INCIVILITY HURTS US AS INDIVIDUAL CITIZENS

Each of us has witnessed our share of uncivil political behavior. Most of us are familiar with the image of the surly politician who trades in personal attacks, innuendos, and put-downs. We've come to identify folks like this as individuals who are actively or passively aggressive, who won't respond to the points we raise or the questions we ask, or who simply won't listen to a word we say. As a result, many of us tune out or choose not to discuss religion *or* politics because the conversation is neither enjoyable nor enlightening.

It's understandable that political conversation can rile people up. Diverging opinions are inescapable in any democracy.[1] Democracies depend on people being engaged; otherwise they cease being worthy of the name. But passion that turns into aggression or simply causes others to check out is another thing. When that happens, all parties lose.

Incivility is, first and foremost, a denial of the respect owed to a fellow citizen. Civility demands that we pay attention to one other. Civility is the proper relation between people who see themselves as equals in a democracy. Incivility is a denial of it, a stance that says: "You don't count." Yet in a true democracy everyone counts, which explains why British philosopher and economist John Stuart Mill considered stifling someone else's opinion to be an "evil." Even if we disagree with another person's perspective, Mill purported, everyone is worthy of having a voice. After all, what good is having a voice if you're whistling in the dark all the time, or if others simply turn a deaf ear? It's no different from having no voice at all.

If the phrase "having no voice at all" reminds you of some of the worst periods in U.S. history, it should. The history of the United States is complex and has involved near-constant struggle and bloody wars. Still, however gradually and grudgingly, Americans have, throughout our nation's history, accorded the dignity all deserve to an ever-widening circle of citizens. Against the long sweep of the American experience, incivility can be seen as a kind of willful backsliding. As Americans, we pride ourselves on not just being tolerant, but also on being accepting of the new, the innovative, and the different. Our history as a nation includes many periods in which we have opened our hearts and minds to new voices. Incivility is, in a sense, a purified form of intolerance, because it rejects all that it is different as unworthy of the minimal respect that would merit serious consideration. One might even call incivility "indiscriminate discrimination"—discrimination that uses only the slightest difference in background, party affiliation, or policy stance as an excuse for writing others off or even for personally attacking them.

If you think about it, telling someone, however subtly, that they don't matter, or that they aren't worth talking to, is against the values this country was built on. Furthermore, if you deny your fellow citizens the floor, why should they grant it to you? Incivility *can and probably should be* returned by civility in most cases, but incivility doesn't *deserve* a civil response, any more than intolerance deserves tolerance.

By contrast, a civil attitude does merit a civil response. Civility begets civility—perhaps the key message of this book. Civility is an attitude of openness to others based on respect. It is, an invitation to interact in ways that do justice both to our shared humanity and to our many differences—in personality, backgrounds, beliefs, hopes, and aspirations. It is an invitation that more often than not will be accepted. The civil person is, in effect, saying, "Because I respect you, I respect what you're saying, even if (perhaps especially if!) I disagree with it." The tacit promise here is a promise to put mutual respect above going for the jugular attack, doing lasting harm, or even scoring points just for the satisfaction of belittling someone else. To go back to the playground analogy, it's a promise to avoid bullying in the name of having fun. Making this promise—and then turning it into a habit—rests in the first instance on the simple recognition that as democratic citizens we have much more to gain from each other by cooperating with one another in a civil manner than in resorting to insults and attacks and running each other down (even if we see ourselves first and foremost as individual citizens).

And just what do we have to gain? Mutual respect, for one. But the answer goes beyond that. If we really mean it when we say "everyone is entitled to their opinion," then we have a duty not only to listen to other people's opinions, but also to come to terms with them. We can't do that without really grappling with them—especially when their opinions disagree with our own. It's easy to come to terms with opinions like our own. That requires minimal or no effort. Civility, however, requires much effort. If we write off or, worse, ridicule those whose opinions differ from our own, all we're doing is saying that we won't seriously consider other perspectives.

Shrugging off or putting down others leads to some negative effects on those on the receiving end. Who likes to be insulted or written off? If you've got thick skin, you'll respond in kind. If you've got thin skin, you'll probably be insulted. In either case, any real exploration of ideas will quickly cease.

All of this may seem obvious. Less obvious, though, is that incivility harms those guilty of it as much as, if not more, than those who find themselves the victims of it. To see how, try this experiment on yourself. First, think of a political question or concern you care deeply about—jobs, abortion, climate change, the national debt, or education—then answer these questions:

▶ Have I considered all dimensions of the question?

▶ Have I thought about the various interests, emotions, and values that enter into my concern about it?

▶ Have I explored a range of possible responses to those interests, emotions, and values?

▶ Have I explored and weighed the most important consequences of those responses?[2]

Learning about ancient societies or frog's innards, or even our jobs, may be something we think we're done with when we take our last test and stop going to school. But if you think about it, for citizens in a democracy, school is never out. As citizens, we all have an obligation to keep learning, essentially, forever. No degree of certainty about our political beliefs can erase this obligation. In the first place, the political landscape is changing at an accelerating pace as the world becomes more technologically and socially complex. As citizens we should all strive to keep up with the changes in our national policy—every bit as much as doctors, lawyers, and accountants need to keep up with changes in their professional fields. Second, it's not only the world that changes. We change as individuals over the course of our lifetimes, too. As we do, we're constantly reshuffling our beliefs, values, and aspirations. Third, even if both the world and our "inner" selves were entirely static, some effort or learning would be required to discover and then defend our "true" self-interest, our most basic social commitments and how these fit together. We also need to continually work at discovering how all of these *might* fit together in the future. In the end, then, knowing "where to stand" is not as simple as it's made out to be. It requires shifting our feet as we grow and adjusting to a changing world. Such shifting and sorting might even be called the citizen's most basic duty; unless this takes place, there can be no careful consideration of alternative courses of action—something tantamount to irresponsibility. Incivility makes discharging that duty and acting responsibly, both for oneself and others, that much harder. Incivility shrinks our options by closing off alternatives; civility expands them by opening our eyes to them.

Despite this, it must be satisfying at some level to silence others. If it weren't, incivility wouldn't be the scourge it has become. Some may do it out of a genuine, if misplaced, belief that they really *know* the answers (which would require that they also really *knew* the right questions!). A few may even do it, ironically, because they're willing to use verbal violence to avoid what they see as a greater risk of physical violence. But these cases probably aren't very typical. Most of the incivility that we all experience, and that scholars have documented, is probably unthinking. More to the point, silencing someone can never be proof that we've earned their respect—or their agreement. Nor can it teach us anything further about the topic at hand. The Uncle, associate, radio personality, or Senator who silences the other person at the table will rejoice in "winning"—all the while losing the very thing we enter conversations to gain: a chance to further our understanding and to learn. Bullies lose out because they diminish themselves by their actions. The uncivil do the same, fencing in their minds in the process.

HOW INCIVILITY HURTS SOCIETY

Law school professors teach their students that the point of the First Amendment is to guarantee everyone a soapbox. But why, in the end, are soapboxes so important? It isn't primarily because those who use them feel better (though they might); it's that having a lot of them is the best way our society can ensure a rich conversation about the problems we face and the opportunities open to us—individually and collectively. Free speech isn't important because it's therapeutic; it's important because the freer it is, the richer it is, and the likelier we are, as citizens and as a society, to fully explore ideas and sort out the good from the bad.[3] A civil society engages in thoughtful exploration. Civility promotes thoughtfulness; incivility inhibits it. This is the second key theme that you will see running through the rest of these pages. Thoughtfulness leads to well-considered questions and answers; thoughtlessness doesn't lead much of anywhere. It's easy to see, then, why civil societies are likely to be smarter than those that aren't. The damage that incivility wreaks on society's efforts to think through its problems is only the beginning. Incivility short-circuits discussion. At the extreme, incivility leads to a near complete breakdown in discussion. Polar opposites replace reasoned exchanges and a search for—and an ability to acknowledge—common ground. Unilateral demands replace open-ended negotiations. Demonizing the opposition becomes the norm. Pundits rant and Congress is gridlocked. The federal government ceases to function and Main Street turns its attention to other things. The ship of state begins to look rudderless, crewless, and clueless.

Some people might rejoice at the idea of a government that's adrift, but a government that's dead in the water isn't much use to anyone, least of all to those who depend on it for protection. The idea of democracy doesn't prescribe that we head in the same direction—only that we stick together as we move forward. Incivility makes that harder. Incivility weakens the ties that hold us together as a democratic nation. The weaker we are, the less we're able to control our collective fate, which takes on greater meaning when you consider the challenges facing our national security, our fiscal stability, climate shocks, health care and social security, and our energy strategy. The second problem with incivility is that in addition to hindering thoughtful public policy, it gets in the way of coherent public policy. Incivility not only makes it harder to explore and adopt the best available policy options, it also makes it harder to adopt any options at all. Incivility makes the Constitution's mandate to "promote the common welfare" that much more difficult.

A third and more insidious problem with incivility is that the more it spreads, the more it is tolerated and the more corrosive it becomes. As it becomes commonplace, it becomes the rule. People begin to think, "That's just the way things are." It becomes a habit and, as habits go, it is probably just as hard to break as any other. In the long term, that's the most ominous threat of all. James Madison begins the most famous treatise written about American politics, *Federalist 10*, by repeating a warning about the danger of factions put forth by his ally, Alexander Hamilton. Madison observed that "removing the causes" of faction can only be accomplished by "destroying liberty" or "giving to every citizen the same opinions, the same passions, and the same interests"—a frightful evocation of *1984* almost two centuries before Orwell's famous depiction of a society of automatons. Yet Madison believed that liberty and diversity could be preserved and the dangers of faction contained—not by abolishing faction, but rather by "controlling its effects." How? By pitting faction against faction. [4] This was the basic design principle Madison enshrined in the U.S. Constitution, of which he was the principal architect. In historic terms, the system has worked remarkably well—but only to the extent that competing factions have remained civil and have chosen to discuss and broker their differences. Remove civility and the sparks that Madison saw as inevitable between factions will no longer illuminate our way, or be adequately buffered by our system of "checks and balances." Remove civility, and the sparks are instead likely to smolder, shrouding our collective endeavors in smoke.

HOW THE INDIVIDUAL AND SOCIAL EFFECTS OF INCIVILITY AGGRAVATE EACH OTHER

Comparing incivility to bullying helps bring home its immediate reality. Comparing it to disease helps bring home some of the ways its effects on individuals and society interact. Incivility, like disease, can be thought of in clinical terms (as doctors do). Alternatively, incivility, like disease, can be thought of in population terms, (as public health professionals do). We alluded to some of the reciprocal effects these have. But we need to look more closely to see what's revealed when we view the effects of each in terms of the other—when, in other words, we look at the clinical effects of incivility through a public health lens and its effects on public health through a clinical lens.

Incivility presents itself "clinically" as disrespect and discrimination on one hand, and self-certainty and an unwillingness to acquire new information or consider alternative opinions on the other. It seems clear that neither sort of individual "symptom" is likely to go away on its own. Disrespect and discrimination don't cure themselves; closed minds don't open all on their own. But is incivility likely to spread if not checked? Yes, by both sorts of "carriers," that is, by those on the giving and receiving ends of uncivil behavior. For those on the giving end, discrimination and disrespect can be perversely enjoyable and therefore self-reinforcing. Bad behavior can spread when others perceive there's something, however morally questionable, to be gained from it. For those on the receiving end of incivility, it's natural to want to fight the fire of uncivil behavior with fire of one's own. Responding to uncivil behavior with civility requires more effort and greater moral fiber than countering a broadside with a broadside of one's own. Incivility encourages irresponsibility, not measured or thoughtful action. This dynamic may go some way toward explaining the "virulence" of incivility. Some find it immediately gratifying, while others who are initially immune to it find their resistance difficult to sustain in the face of repeated attacks. This also suggests an important corollary we would all do well to remember: No one is invulnerable to being enlisted in its cause.

At some point, the spread of incivility begins to affect not just individual citizens but the wider body politic. Society's ability to heal the damage inflicted by incivility is diminished, its ability to stop further infection reduced. It is sometimes difficult to be civil; most of us need reminding from time to time that civility is the high road, that it's both the right path and the path that's in our long-term individual interest. Without such reminders, it becomes harder to remain civil ourselves. So it is that the clinical effects of incivility begin to have effects on public health, which in turn aggravate the clinical effects. As the vicious circle of incivility continues, individuals are hurt, as is society as a whole. Society, too, loses the collective capacity to cope with new challenges, new information, and new possibilities. It loses the ability to learn and apply its learning. Ironically, this imposes a subtle second cost on individuals. As individuals, we lose chances to learn about our self-interest and about our collective interests. If we aren't learning from one another, then we lose doubly—first as "private citizens" then as citizens with social commitments. Then there are the "clinical" side effects of other public health impacts of incivility. The first such public health impact we see is gridlock. Gridlock, whether in government or society at large, gets in the way of getting important things done. We depend on government and other social agencies, groups, and associations for too much. But gridlock has another negative effect. If incivility directly turns people off, gridlock indirectly turns them off. The harder it becomes to work together, whether in government or voluntary associations, the less people will engage in their work and the less they pay attention to it. Again, the individual learning that responsible citizen decision-making depends upon suffers.

If gridlock paralyzes our collective efforts, faction ruptures them, but the effect on learning is the same. When faced with warring factions, individuals will be tempted to either join in or retreat to the safety of their private fortresses. They will be under pressure to protect themselves by responding in kind or

Let's Talk Politics

surrounding themselves with walls. Interaction becomes scary, and learning takes a back seat to peace and quiet or self-preservation.

WHAT'S NEEDED

In the early days of America's history, civil society was a local, hands-on experience. Free, land-owning white men routinely read and even penned political pamphlets and participated in town hall meetings. The fact that the citizenry was alike in terms of class, race, and proximity ensured that politics was largely a matter of face-to-face interaction. Now things are more complex, and the vast majority of us would say that we're glad that's the case. In modern-day America, you don't have to own land or be of the majority population to be actively involved in political life. With this complexity comes friction, but with it also comes a greater richness and variety of experience and thinking.

We've now seen that incivility has negative effects on both individuals and society, and that these effects tend to aggravate each other. We owe it to each other as equal citizens of a democratic society, and to ourselves as individuals with both private and collective aspirations, to do something about them. Incivility isn't merely nasty; it threatens America's most basic values of mutual respect and individual responsibility.[5]

Any attempt at reversing the current spread of incivility in the United States needs to be based on a clear recognition of these dynamics. Since incivility works at both the individual and social level, so too must any effective response. The more a "cure" is able to attack both the clinical and population sources of incivility, the better its chances of success; the more a response can operate at both the individual and social levels, the likelier it is to work. The rest of this book describes just such an antidote to incivility. It outlines how you can contribute by initiating a virtuous circle of civility among those with whom you interact, whether in your church, neighborhood, civic group, or workplace. You'll learn how to promote constructive conversation through exploratory discussion. What you'll find in the chapters to come is less a blueprint for social engineers than a guide for citizens, less a design than a set of tools. In Chapters 5-8, we describe an overall approach for injecting civility into your life—an approach intended to be used in the here-and-now rather than some far-off civil utopia, one that is focused on individual citizens rather than government officials or institutions. And then, in the final chapter, we go one step further by providing you with a set of free resources you can use as you customize that approach to your own circumstances and interests and then implement it.

Our first hope is that by making these tools available, readers will understand that there's a clear alternative to passively accepting incivility and that more constructive conversations are within every citizen's reach. Challenging incivility is not rocket science, though it does require effort, planning, and some attention to technique. If you're willing to learn the ropes, we're confident that the approach and resources we provide here will work for you. We're confident because they've worked for us and for many others, as we explain in Chapter 4. Our second hope, of course, is that by seeing a workable alternative within reach, readers will be encouraged to reach for—and use—it.

The solution we describe beginning in the next chapter has at its core a process of exploratory discussion, a process that encourages civility on both the individual and group levels. This process is neither theoretical nor academic, but practical. It has a proven —and solid—track record, one based on thousands of hours of experience with real citizens and groups of all stripes in virtually all areas of the country. Best of all, we'll explain how *you*—or your group—can put it to use *now* with little more than what you'll learn from this book and the resources it identifies.

If you're ready to roll up your sleeves and start learning the basics of a tried-and-true approach to building civility and reaping its benefits, skip the next chapter and have a look at Chapters 4 and 5. We begin there by detailing the concrete benefits we've gotten from using the exploratory discussion approach we'll be describing later on, not only in terms of civility, but also in terms of our second key theme: thoughtfulness. If you're still hesitant about whether it might be worth trying, or whether there's anything you can add, have a look at Chapter 3. It tackles every objection we could think of to getting involved in the cause of civility. Just remember, to do nothing is to leave the field open to incivility, and, as we've detailed here, that's a choice none of should make lightly.

NOTES

1. As the news magazine *The Economist*, often seen as a champion of private solutions to social problems, explained recently:

    > On a personal level, the state matters because it has a big impact on people's lives. [...] [T]he quality of the state you live in will do more to determine your well-being than natural resources, culture or religion. In the surveys that measure people's happiness, decent government is as important as education, income and health (all of which are themselves dependent on government). (March 19, 2011; p. 6).

2. Most of us would like to answer yes to these questions, but if we are totally honest with ourselves, then it seems highly unlikely that we would have thought so broadly about these concerns. This is where Mill's warning comes in handy. It's a useful reminder that complete certainty is an illusion. Mill didn't invent this notion, nor was he the last to comment on its importance. Scholars will tell you that human fallibility is a cornerstone of virtually every religion and philosophy in history. For all of their differences, they agree on this key point: We humans are capable of knowing the world around

us, but none of us can be a know-it-all. For the origin of, and an extended meditation on, the implications of this insight, see Charles W. Anderson's far-ranging and lively *A Deeper Freedom* (Madison, Wis.: University of Wisconsin Press, 2002).

3. The best, extended statement of this line of thinking probably remains Cass Sunstein's *Democracy and the Problem of Free Speech* (New York: Free Press, 1993).

    The literature on the importance of discussion in democracy more generally extends to Greek antiquity and includes familiar contributors such as American John Dewey. The past generation has witnessed a vibrant renewal of interest in democratic discussion, discourse, and dialogue among both scholars and lay citizens. Those interested in the deeper philosophical and theoretical questions this topic involves would do well to start with any of the recent writings of John Dryzek, particularly his comprehensive and incisive *Deliberative Democracy and Beyond: Liberals, Critics, Contestations* (New York: Oxford University Press, 2000). Those interested in learning more about the nuts and bolts of specific alternatives to the approach we'll be describing in Part II might well start with John Gastil and Peter Levine's *The Deliberative Democracy Handbook* (San Francisco, Cal.: Jossey-Bass, 2005). For a direct comparison of those alternatives to our own approach, see *Public Discussion as the Exploration and Development of Contrasting Conceptual Possibilities*, by Adolf Gundersen; Julius Stern, Ed. (Parkersburg, WV: Interactivity Foundation, 2006, downloadable at: www.interactivityfoundation.org).

4. James Madison, *The Federalist No. 10*. Originally published in *The New York Packet*, Friday, November 23, 1787. Reprinted in Henry S. Commager, Ed. *Selections from The Federalist: Hamilton, Madison, Jay* (Arlington Heights, Ill.: Harlan Davidson: 1949). p. 10.

Let's Talk Politics

As noted in *The Blackwell Encyclopaedia of Political Science*, Vernon Bogdanor, Ed. (Cambridge, Mass.: Basil Blackwell: 1991), Madison built on and contributed to a long tradition that continues into the contemporary period:

> In elaborating the psychological requirements of democratic stability Aristotle spoke of "political friendliness," a sense of "partnership" and "political restraint"; Tocqueville wrote of "self interest rightly understood," "temperance, moderation, and self command"; Bagehot wrote of "animated moderation"; and Eckstein stressed the importance of "balanced disparities" (p. 98).

The same entry goes on to observe that:

> This theory of the psychological components of stable democracy has not been disproven by attitude changes that have occurred in Europe and the United States in recent decades. Political polarization and declining national pride and confidence in Britain and the United States have been associated with the declining effectiveness of the British and American governments and economies […] (p. 99).

5. At least two recent book-length studies have expressed similar concerns: Susan Herbst's *Rude Democracy: Civility and Incivility in American Politics* (Philadelphia, Penn.: Temple University Press, 2010) and Os Guinness's *The Case for Civility: And Why Our Future Depends on It* (New York: HarperOne, 2008).

CHAPTER 2

— Introduction to the IF Approach: Civility Through Exploratory Discussion

In this chapter, we present an approach to discussing politics that, on the surface, does not look especially unusual or unique. A small group of five to eight people gather over a meal to talk politics. Looking more closely, however, public discussions held by the Interactivity Foundation (IF) are unique in both their purpose, materials, process, and organization. At its heart, IF's discussion process is a carefully developed and tested approach to discussing emergent political issues. And that's a good thing—because it means that non-professionals can put this approach to work for themselves, as long as they develop a decent sense of how it works. Indeed, the beauty of the IF process is that it is robust enough to be forgiving. You don't have to be a seasoned veteran or a facilitating guru to participate.

As we fill in the details of this more intentional approach to discussion, we'll be paying special attention to the multiple reasons the IF approach might be expected to promote civility.[1] Chapter 5 provides plenty of evidence, based on the experiences of more than 1,000 IF discussion participants, that confirms these expectations.

A QUICK OVERVIEW OF THE IF APPROACH TO EXPLORATORY PUBLIC DISCUSSIONS

The IF process developed from a West Virginia banker's efforts to improve the practice of American democracy. Julius "Jay" Stern was born on the eve of World War I, the eldest son of a banking family. Jay was expected to shepherd the banking interests of his family when he came of age. Jay, however, was a philosopher. And although he had a brief opportunity to study philosophy at the Massachusetts Institute of Technology and Harvard, Jay remained a banker and businessman for most of his life. Still, he never abandoned his interest in philosophy or the ways he could apply it to politics. Until he died at age 95, he continued to log 60-hour weeks to further the mission of the foundation he had created.[2]

Late in his life, Jay developed a means by which everyday citizens could work with experts to flesh out a set of policy approaches to an area of political concern. The report resulting from that work could then later be explored by other small groups of citizens. Jay envisioned this approach as a means of providing "staff work" to citizens. Just as politicians have staff to research various policy approaches, citizens could benefit from the efforts of other citizens working with experts to develop exploratory reports on any number of emergent policy-related concerns—before these concerns became political crises. The resulting reports would give groups of everyday citizens both the encouragement and a useful starting point for exploring policy-related issues. As such, citizens could become better-informed participants in their democracy.

This idea eventually grew into a small, private, nonpartisan foundation called the Interactivity Foundation, or "IF." More than just creating better-informed citizens, however, IF discussions provide safe spaces in which citizens can practice civility. The result is more engaged citizens who have a deeper capacity to genuinely engage and appreciate different political perspectives. This guide invites you to use IF reports to create your own exploratory discussion forums, and this chapter explains how IF reports emerge and the ways they can generate lively and engaged small-group discussions. Further details about how you can set up your own discussions can be found in the second section of this guide.

PROCESS AND ORGANIZATION

One of the things that distinguishes IF discussions is the reports we use and the means by which they are developed. Facilitators working with one small group of expert-specialists and another of citizen-generalists create the reports. Including expert-specialists ensures that the reports incorporate conceptual-level thinking and cutting-edge ideas relevant to the topic being explored. Including citizen-generalists ensures that the reports stay focused on the big picture, that they speak to lay citizens' concerns, and that they do so in a way that lay citizens can readily grasp. The two panels spend dozens of hours working separately and then come together at the end of the process with the same goal in mind: developing materials that best stimulate exploratory discussions.

The origin of IF's reports—the "how"—is also important. Their "authors" (the panelists) work in sanctuary, which means that they remain anonymous. This has two advantages: First, it frees panelists to say what's really on their minds. Second, it means that users of IF's reports are prevented from getting sidetracked into fruitless arguments over "who said what" in the report. The contents of IF reports stand or fall on their own merit, which means that the ideas they present take priority over personalities. We've found that this model is ideal for having productive discussions. The key steps of the IF discussion process mirror the main sections of IF's discussion reports. Discussions, for example, start with an exploration of participants' concerns (first participants' own concerns, then those presented in the report) and then move on to consider various conceptual policy responses to those concerns. They conclude by examining the possible consequences of these responses. There's nothing particularly complicated about this process: possible concerns, possible responses, possible consequences. This three-step process is probably similar to what many of us employ when faced with difficult and important personal decisions.

Consider the following scenario, which countless Americans encounter daily[3]:

> *Your spouse or partner receives a job offer in a distant city. It's a good position, and the city is attractive and interesting. But the move will mean spending significantly less time with your extended family and friends.*

The question is how do we go about making good decisions? No book or online source can tell you what to do. Expert advice will only take you so far. At some point, after which you've hashed and rehashed the decision with your partner or spouse, you'll may get that gnawing feeling that you are missing something, that you need to step back and get a fresh perspective (maybe more than one). And at about that time you may to call on others to help you "think this thing through."

You'd likely seek out people who could provide you with new insight rather than those who are more apt to *tell* you what to do. Sometimes by direct invitation and sometimes simply as a result of explaining yourself to others, your conversations will widen and the process will give new life to the discussions you have at home. By the time you're done, your decision—though still your own—will be informed by the other people you've consulted. No matter what you decide, you'll feel better about where you land because you've relied on others to help you explore your full range of options.

What do such decisions look like? No big secret there either. We've all made them. You don't spend a lot of time on details; the bigger the choice, the less the details matter since they can't be predicted. If they're about life-altering situations, they'll usually begin with some very basic questions such as, "What do I really care about?" and "What do I want out of life?" They'll also probably include an attempt to sketch out all available options, or all of the possibilities. And they'll almost inevitably involve a discussion of the likely consequences to the extent that you can foresee them. So it turns out that most of us have had plenty of experience in our private lives with an informal decision-making process. That process mirrors what takes place during an IF exploratory discussion of public policy.

Let's get back to the core steps of the IF process: possible concerns, possible responses, possible consequences. Each of these stress variety, alternatives, and contrast, for it is by examining a range of outcomes that we gain the most insight and best identify common ground—even when it appears that none exists. When all that we see are Idea A and Idea B, it can be hard to imagine others. But if we are exposed to Ideas C, D, E, F, and G, we might find that we could agree on Idea E—especially if it were combined with some version of Idea G.

Why such an emphasis on *possibilities*?[4] The main reason is because thinking about and discussing public policy in terms of possibilities encourages exploration in several important and interactive ways. Possibilities:

▶ are open-ended so they invite continuing discussion and revision

▶ require variety (a "singular possibility" is a contradiction in terms)

▶ allow more internal complexity to the extent that they contrast, complement, and interconnect with one another

▶ encourage everyone to keep the discussion at the conceptual level of "what might be" rather than at the level of more immediate problem solving or policy "fixes"

One final note about the IF process. You might be wondering how IF's discussions deal with potentially disruptive emotions.[5] The answer may come as a surprise. IF's discussion processes are designed to give participants a safe outlet. Rather than assuming that emotions can be ignored or put in a box, the IF process starts from the view that emotions are central to the human experience. Consequently, it treats them as something to be explored rather than censured. Bringing emotions into the discussion lends them the respect they deserve as an important part of what makes us who we are. It also tends to have a series of important and positive side effects. Exploring emotions in a direct way helps prevent them from boiling over and both energizes and enriches IF's discussions. Ironically, by encouraging participants to examine their full range of emotions about a particular policy, IF's process produces discussions that are more "reasonable" and, hence, more civil.

As we've outlined, the IF process is robust, but it works best when set in the appropriate context—one that is relaxed, casual, and neighborly. To encourage that kind of setting, IF public discussions almost always include a meal (and cover transportation and child care costs).[6] They also feature small groups—from five to eight (at most 10) citizens—so participants can really get to know one another yet don't feel the need to defend themselves, score points, or play to the crowd. Finally, because they last anywhere from four to eight hours on average, participants have plenty of time to dig into the discussion material without feeling rushed. The process emphasizes possibilities, concepts, and contrasts—already modeled in the discussion materials— all of which promote civility. So, too, do the various organizational features of IF's public discussion: small groups, a shared meal, and a relaxed pace (four to eight hours). Although it is possible to hold an IF discussion online, our experience makes us partial to face-to-face dialogue. It optimizes and encourages a certain type of decorum while making it harder to avoid, dismiss, or discount conflicting views. When everyone is sitting together in a classroom or a church basement or sharing a meal around a dinner table, it is much harder to write off other participants or their ideas. Perhaps this is why Jesus, Buddha, and other religious figures reportedly broke bread with both their followers and detractors. Meals break the ice, but their real importance lies in reminding everyone of our shared humanity. They are a congenial, lived reminder that, on some basic level, we are all the same even while our opinions may differ. A relaxed pace is likewise crucial to the success of IF's public discussions. Four hours is about the minimum participants will need to fully explore concerns, possibilities, and consequences, particularly if they want to make good use of the preparatory materials that are available. An unhurried tempo contributes to the exploratory tone of the discussion by freeing participants to follow up on one another's comments, build on one another's ideas, and pursue new perspectives.

All of this may be a lot to take in, so we've provided the following summary table. It identifies how each of the features of IF public discussions contributes to civility:

IF PUBLIC DISCUSSION FEATURE	HOW IT ENCOURAGES CIVILITY
Process Feature	
Possibilities & concerns—not recommendations or advocacy	▶ No definitive or final perspective is possible, so discussion is kept open
Broad concerns & directions—not narrow technical questions & answers	▶ Deters advocacy
Contrasts or alternatives—not "the right answers"	▶ Encourages exploration ▶ Disagreement is *always* acceptable
Organizational Feature	
Small face-to-face groups	▶ Encourage interaction
Shared meal	▶ Promotes respect for others' ideas
Unhurried pace	▶ Encourages exploration

Table 2.1. How the Process and Organization of Interactivity Foundation Public Discussions Promote Civility[7]

Each of the aspects of an IF discussion described in Table 2.1, sometimes singularly but more often working in some combination, helps reinforce the exploratory purpose of IF discussions while counteracting competition and argument. In other words, each step in the process, as well as the setting in which it takes place, simultaneously discourages incivility and encourages civility. More specifically, the steps in the process and the organizational setting prevent individual participants from feeling as if they must emerge as the "winner" or that they must agree with one another. Participants also work toward encouraging other discussants to view their differences, variety of perspectives, and alternative viewpoints as not just acceptable but desirable. The net result is that participants are more willing to voice and consider new ideas. When citizens begin to take on the role of co-explorers in this way, the circle of civility is widened both directly, as participants expand their vision, and indirectly, as they gain an appreciation for their co-explorers who helped them do so.

PURPOSES

Getting a better feel for how alternative policy directions differ—and why—is the kind of understanding that can provide a firm foundation for civility. IF's public discussions require no group agreement or consensus as to what policy ought to do or how it ought to work. However, the organization's ultimate goal of clarifying choices is accomplished principally by having participants carefully work together to consider multiple concerns and possible responses to them, an activity that tends to serve the goal of civility. Although it might seem that civility is thus a by-product of the IF process, it is no less true that IF's mission of "enhanced choice" depends on participants seeing alternative choices as authentic and worthy of consideration, which, in turn, requires seeing those who hold those views as authentic and worthy of consideration. The widened alternatives on which IF public discussions depend thus go hand in hand with greater civility. Indeed, the one presupposes the other.[8]

GUIDELINES

Although IF's discussions require no group consensus upon any particular policy approach, the discussion's guidelines need to be worked out in advance. Usually, it's simply a matter of explaining that in order for exploration to work, cooperation and creativity have to take priority over competition or the need to be right. We've found that it helps to spell out the "discussion rules" and get participants to explicitly acknowledge them. It can also work for the facilitator to specify one or two guidelines to start and then to let the group brainstorm about what they might add.

Different IF facilitators use different sets of rules, guidelines, or contracts. The following list of "rules" was adapted from a list developed by IF's President, Jack Byrd, Jr.[9]

These ground rules are intended to ensure that we help others explore and develop their own thinking.

1. We will be *positive*. We will offer *alternatives* that *build on* each other's insights and not simply tear down or negate others' ideas.

2. We will be *open* to each other and will try to avoid persuading others to take our point of view.

3. We will contribute when we can offer new insights, but we will try to *avoid repeating* what has already been said.

4. We will avoid story telling and personal experience sharing except when we can *connect them to the broader aspects* of the possibilities.

5. We will *feel free* to share our thoughts even when they might not be fully developed.

Notice that all of these rules (to the extent they're followed) promote civility. They aren't just about playing nice; they encourage participants to actively explore a broad discussion rather than ignore disagreements. Being positive and open, avoiding repetition, and feeling open to sharing even partially formed ideas encourage participants to focus on ideas rather than personalities—and to do so in an accepting and supportive way. Furthermore, the rules stress keeping an open mind, building on others' ideas, and offering contrasts or alternatives, all while avoiding the temptation to persuade others to take our side.

Occasionally, of course, facilitators—like any referee—need to remind participants of the rules. That's why it's good to discuss them before things get underway (and perhaps even have participants sign an agreement to abide by them). But enforcing the rules is far from the only thing IF facilitators do. In fact, as we'll discuss later, facilitators are in some ways the most crucial element of a successful discussion, despite the fact that they don't directly contribute to it.

MATERIALS

Another important reason IF's public discussions tend to yield civil exchanges, as opposed to a heated debate, involves the published materials that are used as a starting points. Table 2.2 presents in summary form how IF's discussion reports differ from typical reports on public policy.

	TYPICAL POLICY REPORTS	IF PUBLIC DISCUSSION REPORTS
WHAT	Analysis of a problem Recommendations for solutions	Areas of concern Divergent, contrasting possibilities Possible outcomes or consequences
WHY	To make or influence immediate decisions	To provide a starting point for an exploratory discussion
WHO	Experts and representatives of interest groups	Expert-specialists and citizen-generalists
HOW	Public discussions Decisions made by compromise or consensus	In "sanctuary" Freedom to speak openly Focusing on ideas, not personalities or participants' interests Emphasis upon providing contrasting approaches to thinking about policy—not upon decision or consensus

Table 2.2. Interactivity Foundation Reports: A Way to Start Discussions, Not Settle Arguments[10]

It's easy to see how the elements listed in the right-hand column might help curtail incivility, all while helping to keep the discussion moving in an exploratory direction. Earlier we commented upon the "what" and "how" of the contents of IF reports and how they relate to the IF process, but other features of IF's reports are equally important, such as the way in which discussions are framed.

Participants don't have to slavishly study IF reports or spend a lot of time on the particulars for the reports to make a positive contribution. What's important is that the reports convey *how* IF discussions are supposed to work, what they're supposed to focus on, and at what level—and then offer several potential avenues of discussion. In other words, the role of the report is not to inform participants about what they should be discussing, but rather model the kind of open-ended thinking that the discussions seek to promote.

Currently, IF has a catalogue of more than two dozen discussion reports covering areas of concern that include education, energy, democratic renewal, and retirement. (A full list can be found in Chapter 6 of this guide.) The reports are free and can be obtained from the Foundation or by downloading them from IF's Website.

FACILITATION

IF facilitators direct the discussion; they don't control it. Their job isn't to explore the report themselves but to ensure that participants do so by following the discussion rules. By paying attention to the discussion materials and sticking to the discussion process, facilitators do much more than simply exclude uncivil behavior; they actively promote and model civility.

All of this may sound like a tall order, but you don't have to be a professional to get the job done. In Chapter 7, we'll show you where to go if you're interested in learning some of the tricks of the trade, but being a good IF facilitator comes down to a few key elements:

- ▶ Each participant understands the discussion guidelines—and sticks to them

- ▶ The discussion stays on topic and keeps moving

- ▶ Participants' own interests, emotions, and concerns aren't ignored but are used as fuel for further exploration

All of these ensure that the focus stays squarely on alternative ways of thinking about a specific concern, promoting a civil discussion, and conferring legitimacy upon each participant and their perspectives. They say loudly and clearly: "Your thoughts matter."

TAKING DEMOCRACY SERIOUSLY

At their core, the various design elements of IF public discussions work toward the same end: making sure that people interact constructively. A successful IF discussion isn't one in which everyone has equal say. The rules, facilitator, materials, and process all demand more than that, specifically that participants pay active attention to what one another is saying. The group works to build a constructive, vigorous, respectful democratic conversation.[11] When it works, which is more often than not, civility isn't just promoted, it's practiced, modeled, and achieved. And when civility reigns, the rule "of, by, and for the people" becomes the rule "of, by, and for the people who work together, even with those with whom they disagree." That's the promise of IF's public discussions. Learning to have real, democratic conversations across political and ideological lines requires opportunities to practice that kind of exchange. Now, let's go on to explore what keeps some people from engaging in political discussions and why they might find IF discussions unique, compelling, and effective opportunities to have useful conversations about politics.

NOTES

1. For a book-length version of this chapter's contents, see Adolf G. Gundersen, *Public Discussion as the Exploration and Development of Contrasting Conceptual Possibilities*. Report published by the Interactivity Foundation, Parkersburg, WV, November 2006: http://www.interactivityfoundation.org/resources-downloads/papers.

2. *Julius "Jay" Stern 1913–2009: A Biography.* A lively and personal biography of IF founder Jay Stern. Natalie Hopkinson. 2010. Parkersburg, WV: Interactivity Foundation. Available at no cost in printed form directly from IF. Mail request to P.O. Box 9; Parkersburg, West Virginia; 26102-0009. Also downloadable directly from the IF Website (see above).

3. The following section incorporates material originally published in *Public Discussion: We've All Done It Before* on the Interactivity Foundation Website (www.interactivityfoundation.org), posted January 14, 2010.

4. Ibid., *Possibilities and Exploratory Discussion*, on the Interactivity Foundation Website (www.interactivityfoundation.org), posted July 20, 2010.

5. Ibid., *A Little Emotion Goes a Reasonably Long Way* on the Interactivity Foundation Website (www.interactivityfoundation.org), posted October 14, 2010. The emotional flexibility of the IF process goes a long way, we believe, toward meeting psychological critiques of "rationality" or deliberation. For one such critique, see Jonathan Haaidt's 2012 book *The Righteous Mind: Why Good People Are Divided by Politics and Religion*. New York: Pantheon Books.

6. See Chapter 6 for some creative ideas about how you might incorporate meals and child care into your discussions, as well as tips on choosing locations that will be broadly accessible.

7. Adapted from Table U-3.1. "How IF Citizen Staff Work Reports Can Stimulate and Enhance Democratic Discussions" in *Public Discussions as the Exploration and Development of Contrasting Possibilities.* Published by the Interactivity Foundation, Parkersburg, WV, November 2006: http://www.interactivityfoundation.org/resources-downloads/papers, p. 106.

8. It is also true that participants will tend to begin to see the larger point that the existence of multiple alternatives further implies that not even any set of alternatives can be considered exhaustive. IF's public discussions thus tend to have a civilizing ripple effect.

9. For a more descriptive example, see "Attachment A—Discussion Guidelines," in *Facilitation Guidebook for Small Group Citizen Discussions, Second Edition.* Jack Byrd, Jr. (Adolf G. Gundersen and Sue Goodney Lea, Editors). Interactivity Foundation, Parkersburg, West Virginia, July 2009: http://www.interactivityfoundation.org/resources-downloads/, p.30.

10. Adapted from Adolf Gundersen, ed. *Health Care: The Case of Depression.* 3rd Edition. Interactivity Foundation, Parkersburg, WV. March 2006. For an expanded analysis of the use of IF's discussion reports, see *Public Discussion as the Exploration and Development of Contrasting Conceptual Possibilities.* Report published by the Interactivity Foundation, Parkersburg, WV, November 2006: http://www.interactivityfoundation.org/resources-downloads/papers, pp. 8-10, 21-4, 106.

11. For a more fully developed version of this line of thinking, see *Public Discussion as the Exploration and Development of Contrasting Conceptual Possibilities.* Report published by the Interactivity Foundation, Parkersburg, WV, November 2006: http://www.interactivityfoundation.org/resources-downloads/papers, pp. 110-14.

CHAPTER 3

— Promoting Civility: No Reason to Sit on the Sidelines

Even if you're convinced that civility is good for the country, you might be wondering: What's in it for me? Getting involved in politics is a lot like eating vegetables—you know they're good for you, but you'd just as soon pass. We're not going to lecture you to get you involved in politics; we just want to whet your appetite for exploratory public discussion—an especially enriching and enjoyable form of "talking politics." But we'd like you to pause for a minute and ask yourself why you'd rather sit on the sidelines. Chances are, you'll recognize your answer in the pages that follow. Each entry begins with a specific objection to "getting involved," voiced by a particular kind of person.[1] Our goal isn't to prove that IF's exploratory discussions are all things to all people, but rather that they can contribute something important to all—or at least most—people. The next couple of chapters describe the increasingly successful experience we've had with the IF discussion process.

WHY PEOPLE STAY ON THE POLITICAL SIDELINES—AND WHY THEY SHOULD MAKE AN EXCEPTION TO GIVE IF DISCUSSIONS A TRY

Strange as it may sound, the descriptions of views in this chapter represent people who are both fictional *and* real. They're fictional in the sense that they are at least partially our inventions. But they are also real in the sense that they embody common objections to participating in political discussion (or even politics as a whole) that we've all heard before. We take these objections quite seriously because they're all reasonable in one sense or another.

"Politics is for Those Who Don't Have to Worry about Putting Bread on the Table"

I've really never been that aware of what's going on in politics. It's not that I'm not interested; it's just that I've always been too busy looking for work—or doing it. Right now, I'm lucky: I've got a good job, and for the first time in years, I'm putting a little money aside each week. The little free time I have, I give to my kids or to just recharging my batteries.

For many people, engaging in public policy discussions seems like a luxury, but it needn't be.[2] We know from experience that organizers can make it easier for potential participants by providing food, transportation, and even child care. (Based on this experience, we'll be providing some suggestions for creative—but simple and inexpensive—ways to deal with these practical needs when we come to the subject of preparing for an IF discussion in Chapter 6.) Even if you're pressed for time, there are some immediate benefits you'll get from participating in an IF discussion: fellowship, a shared meal, and some serious social interaction.[3] Pretty soon we expect that you'll find the small time commitment required of IF discussions is more than made up for by the opportunity they provide for citizens to explore how public policy might contribute to a less-stressed world. IF's public discussions won't solve all your problems, but they're a great place to start thinking about everyone's concerns and how to address them.

"Politics Just Feels Rigged"

I don't know why anyone even thinks of getting involved in politics in any way. I don't buy into conspiracy theories, but how can average people like me compete against big corporations, business groups, and unions—not to mention Wall Street? Hardly a day goes by that someone's not reporting another story about the influence of money on elections or the power of lobbyists. Did Scott Walker defeat his historic recall in Wisconsin in 2012 because he outspent his rival eight to one? Does my local teachers' union have a stranglehold over the school board? I don't know, but I'm more than a bit suspicious and not at all sure that they don't. It all just turns me off. In civics class, we learned that the founding fathers believed that "all men are created equal." I agreed then and I agree now, but I wonder how relevant that is nowadays. I don't have millions to throw around to make my voice heard. It seems like it would take major changes to level the playing field. Until that happens, I'd rather sit on the sidelines.

Unfortunately, there's more truth to this lament than we'd care to admit. When it comes to politics in America, money talks—and more so than in other countries.[4] The ideal of equality is not to blame. In fact, without the ideal of a level playing field, we wouldn't be able to measure how close or distant we are from where we want to be. And we've undoubtedly made progress. Voting and other civil rights have expanded over the last several decades. Educational opportunities have broadened, and, more recently, the Internet has greatly expanded citizens' effective "right to be heard." But continued progress toward full political equality[6] is not likely to occur without real effort. Consequently, those of us who suspect that American politics isn't as fair as it should be are faced with a real dilemma. The situation makes us want to sit on the sidelines, but it won't improve if we do. One of the key contributions exploratory discussion can make to public life is to break through this hopelessness and passivity, not by riling people up, but rather by getting them involved with people they trust—their friends, neighbors, and coworkers—and starting a form of involvement that energizes citizens.

IF's exploratory discussions have various features that ensure that they're kept free and open to everyone who joins in. The rules are the same for all. There is a "facilitator" to make sure they're followed. And because they're aimed at exploring a topic and various ways of thinking about it, no one person can lay claim to the "right answer." As a result, IF's discussions strongly resist manipulation—even by garden-variety loudmouths. By providing participants with the opportunity to learn how other people think about politics, they can also help citizens recognize and resist manipulation of their own ideas.

"Even Political Talk is Just a Clever Way to Keep Us in Line"

> It's not that politics is a pack of lies. The problem isn't propaganda. If it were all about misinformation, the right information would fix things. All we'd need would be for some media watchdogs or whistleblowers to just get out "the facts" and everything would be okay. The problem is deeper than that. No amount of facts can change how we see or understand the world. In politics, it's always a question of who has the most power. Those are people who are in a position to put a "spin" on what's going on. Not many people are in that position. So if you don't have the power to spin the news, all you can do is resist the spin others put on it. All I can do is to try to keep my guard up and be skeptical. As for other people, I guess all I can do is encourage them to be skeptical, too.

This confession would make a certain John Philpot Curran proud—but only to a point. He's the Irish orator and politician who gets the credit for saying, "Eternal vigilance is the price of freedom."[5] But there's a difference between vigilance and cynicism. Much of life in a democracy is a struggle over how important concepts and values are understood. But throwing in the towel to avoid the struggle won't protect you from the powers that be. It will only leave them less fettered and you more isolated. IF exploratory discussions cannot guarantee that you or anyone else will be the wizard behind the curtain, but they are first-rate tools for challenging conventional thinking of all types. They begin with multiple, contrasting, and sometimes innovative starting points. They bring together different sorts of people, and that encourages diverging perspectives, which is a small but significant starting point.

"Politics is Dirty"

> *Whenever I think of politics, scandals, backroom deals, and corruption come to mind. Nothing good ever seems to come out of politics. Sure, government does some things right, but mostly by accident it seems. I know we need government, so political parties and lobbyists are inevitable. But politics seems to reward the lowest-common-denominator sort of behavior. People may enter politics with good intentions, but they don't seem to be able to maintain them for very long. The combined temptations of power and money are just too much. Politics is a necessary evil. I try to avoid the whole thing as much as possible.*

Fair enough. Given the broad sweep of human history, not to mention the constant parade of unsavory characters we're forced to put up with on the news, it's easy to see why someone might want to avoid being "contaminated" by politics. But consider George Washington, Abraham Lincoln, Martin Luther King, Nelson Mandela, and other statesmen and women who have acted honorably and competently. Or, how about something closer to home? At some time in our lives, many of us get involved in a group, organization, or club. In those settings, we are called upon to act like "citizens" in that we must consider, make, and implement decisions that affect other people. The only difference is that rather than acting as a member of a political entity, we're acting as a member of a "private" collective defined by some other shared purpose.[7] In truth, many of us happily plunge into these other "political" forums even while remaining leery of formal or official parties, elections, and the like.

IF exploratory discussions incorporate some of the features of the best of voluntary organizations. They are respectful and orderly, but they also exercise the mind, prepare one to make choices as a citizen, and provide welcome social interactivity. For these reasons, a majority of our participants have said that they would participate in another IF discussion series—and many have. Our discussions are serious, and that is precisely what makes them such good fun.

"Why Can't Everyone Just Get Along?"

> *My reaction to political issues is that people act too much like squabbling children. The world is a big enough place. As a nation, we have enough resources to go around. If people just got along, incivility would disappear.*

True, but that's a very big "if," so big, in fact, that we challenge you to point to any political system throughout human history that resembled a harmonious family for very long. The fact is, each human being is unique, and each of us has different needs, interests, purposes, and ideas of what's desirable. So even when harmony reigns, decisions have to be made. The need for taking stock and exploring options never really goes away, even in the best of times. We just think that discussion is a particularly good way to go about it.

If we turn a blind eye to the differences that exist among us, we lose. If we pretend that all is well, we risk having others shape policies that threaten our democracy by fostering discord,

Let's Talk Politics

disunity, and even hate. Moreover, we lose the opportunity to use our differences as fuel for mutual learning.

"Politics is Too Complicated for Me"

My problem with getting involved in a serious political discussion is simple: It's so complicated that it's over my head. I'm totally intimidated by the issues. Most, such as global warming or education, are topics that experts don't agree on. I don't see how I could contribute. It's hard enough to know whom to vote for.

Again, we agree. In fact, the IF approach to exploratory public discussions was developed with just this problem in mind. How can ordinary citizens deal with the complexity of public policy? One answer might be to throw our hands up and "leave it to the experts." The problem with this answer is that the moment we do that we cease being a democracy and start being an "expert-ocracy" ruled not by the people, but by those with special knowledge. The answer that orients IF public discussions is at once radical and traditional: Focus on the big picture, then leave the details to the experts. It's a radical idea in that we tend to think of citizenship as an all-or-nothing affair: Either you're "informed" or you're not. But who can really be adequately informed on even a slice of public policy? Better to spend time getting a clear survey of the forest first. It's a traditional idea in that it resembles both the relationship among citizens and our government representatives and between the more "generalist" representatives in the legislative branch and the more "specialist" members of the executive branch.

IF exploratory discussions focus on "the big picture" from beginning to end. They explore concerns, possibilities for addressing them, and their consequences at a general level. You don't have to be a scientist or a professional to participate. (In fact, we've found that "ordinary" citizens tend to be better at our process than experts because they naturally keep their eyes on the forest rather than forever wandering into the trees!)

You don't even have to "know" anything about the topic beyond having a sense that it's worth talking about, so lacking expert knowledge is no disadvantage in IF discussions. What really counts in IF's exploratory discussions is a willingness to think through general alternatives with others, not to have specific answers. And where there's that kind of will, the IF process will provide the way.

"I'm Just Too Old for That Sort of Thing"

> *I used to discuss politics quite often when I was younger, but as I've gotten older, I've mostly given up. I'm still interested, but I don't think I could keep up my end of the discussion.*

We sympathize—but only so far, since we've held IF discussions with 70-, 80-, and even 100-year-olds. Most found the discussions enjoyable and informative. IF discussions offer intellectual stimulation and social interaction in addition to their function as "continuing civic self-education"—benefits that seniors tend to appreciate even more than younger participants.

"I'm Just One Person—What Can I Do?"

> *I've never understood why anyone gets involved in politics, campaigns, protests, or these discussions you're talking about. As if I can change anything! I'm just one person. How can I influence anything as large as public policy? It's just too big. It's not that I have anything against politics, but I'd rather accept things as they are and concentrate on things I can change, such as what's going on around me at work, at home, and in my community.*

Politics can make us feel small and powerless. In addition, living in a democracy can paradoxically heighten feelings of powerlessness, because political equality (to the extent it exists) means dispersed power. Only monarchs and emperors have a palpable and immediate impact on events. In democracies, citizens have to join forces to have influence.

IF's exploratory discussions help counteract the feelings of paralysis that so many of us experience when we think about the big challenges of our time. Their first contribution is to strip such concerns of their impenetrability. IF's discussions won't make anyone an expert, but they often achieve something more important: a working knowledge of what's at stake regarding a particular concern and a solid understanding of various ways it might be addressed. Second, by exploring various responses to the concern under discussion, they suggest alternative paths by which citizens can join together to affect the course of public policy. IF's discussions thus transform the overwhelming into something that can be dealt with first in thought and then in action.

"Politics Always Changes Things for the Worse"

Government, politics, public policy—they've always struck me as changing too much too fast. And it's not only that. Whenever I discuss politics, people try to change my position. I don't think change is very often for the good, and I don't like it when people try to change my mind, either.

We couldn't agree more with both of these points. Change may be inevitable, but it always makes sense to ask what's worth fighting to preserve. No one appreciates being lectured by people who are themselves incapable of listening. One of the biggest strengths of the IF discussion process is that it provides ample space to explore change and the various responses to it. Another is that IF facilitators ensure "active listening" and collaborative discussion. IF discussion participants don't just take turns; they're expected to help each other make the most of all of the ideas being discussed and not just the one with which they agree.

"Frankly, Politics is Beneath Me"

I agree with what Winston Churchill said about democracy: It's the best form of government, but only because all of the alternatives are worse. There's nothing very noble or uplifting about it. I'm glad someone chooses to get involved because someone's got to take care of the messy job of governing. Someone has to make sure that the garbage gets collected, and that the police get paid. As for me, I've got better things to do. I play sports, and I like music. I also do volunteer work. I imagine a lot of other people have their own private pursuits and hobbies that they think are important. In any case, isn't improving oneself—however you define that—the most important thing you can do? Politics only seems to get in the way of that.

We would be the last to argue that self-improvement isn't valuable. After all, between the two of us, we've spent close to 30 years trying to encourage it in various educational settings. But if there's one thing we've learned as educators, it's that discussion with peers can be a great way to learn about all kinds of things—provided, of course, that the discussion is well organized. Does exploratory discussion of the kind described in greater detail in the rest of this book meet those standards? We have close to 1,000 responses from past participants that say "yes." Most have said "a great deal."[8] Why? Perhaps the answer is that even the smartest among them—the ones with most to "teach" and least to "learn"—grasp the truth of the old saying, "To teach is to learn twice." The variety of possibilities covered in IF discussions and the variety of those who participate simply make exploration easier. So, far from getting in the way of self-improvement through demanding mental effort, IF's exploratory discussions represent a rare opportunity to pursue it. And, though focused on public policy, they cover a wide array of topics, including philosophy, theology, art, ethics, and sports.

"Politics is Arbitrary"

> I'm not against politics, but I've never seen the attraction, either. I've never felt really committed to a particular party or side of an issue. If you look closely enough, the flowery words and nice speeches are all pretty much the same. I mean, no one can really prove that one policy is better than another. I don't see how they could. Doesn't it all just come down to individual opinion? If so, what difference does it make if my opinion is basically that I don't really care if I have an opinion in the first place?

We doubt many people would maintain this point of view if their neighbor's "opinions" led them to start doing really nasty things. Still, we'd be the first to admit that public policy poses plenty of problems. But isn't the very lack of "proof" that any one policy is better than another all the more reason to keep asking questions and exploring alternative answers? Perhaps the best we can do in most cases is to explore the answers that are available and ask which seems "most" true. We may not discover "the" truth this way, but aren't we likelier to find "our" truth?

IF's approach to exploratory public discussion isn't designed to produce truth or even a set of truths (or answers or recommendations). Instead, it's intended to provide a means for participants to deepen and sharpen their own truth by exploring a range of questions and answers and their consequences. This last bit is important. Exploring the consequences of alternative paths will help you appreciate what might be at stake in following each. That process will not only clarify the choices, but it will also make them more real.

"I Get All the Politics I Need Online"

> *Exploratory political discussion sounds cool, but I already do a lot of that online. I blog a lot and spend a fair amount of time on social networking sites. I like being able to pick and choose from a variety of ideas and forums on the Web. Plus, the convenience of being at home can't be beat. I can't see the benefit of spending a lot of time going out to meetings.*

It sounds like you might be mistaking quantity of information for insight or perspective. Sure, going online can saturate you with information faster than ever before, but is that enough? Don't you also need alternative views and perspectives, analysis, and insights? [9]

Don't get us wrong. We're hardly against online tools, and we've already run a number of discussions online, but whether online or in person, IF's discussions are distinctive in several ways. Most of these characteristics have been mentioned in our previous responses and include:

▶ Guidelines that emphasize the importance of being civil, constructive, and creative

▶ Facilitators who ensure that the guidelines are followed and that the discussion stays coherent and on topic

▶ A process that requires participants to explore alternative framings of the topic and multiple responses to it

▶ These features promote civility both online and off. Online, they have proven to insulate IF's public discussions from what is probably the single most common manifestation of online incivility: "flaming" (or engaging in online arguments by resorting to unfounded personal attacks). [10]

"But We Already Use Our Own Form of Political Discussion"

Political discussions come in a lot of "flavors." There are a lot of models, approaches, and processes out there from which to choose. I've been involved in some already and I was pretty happy with how they went. Why would I want to try changing them?

Not changing them, perhaps, but complementing them. IF's approach is intentionally exploratory, which means it can be easily wed to other processes, as a preliminary stage or step. For example, mediators might use the IF approach as a way to curb conflict by multiplying possibilities. And even where a group, organization, or agency already employs exploratory discussion, IF's approach can sometimes prove a useful addition since it is intentionally general—aimed at eliciting fundamental concerns and questions and the possibilities for addressing them. We believe that many different kinds of discussion have a place in our democracy. We're just asking you to consider trying ours on for size, because it's enjoyable and relatively easy to do.

CONCLUSION

The IF approach doesn't work well in large crowds; it can't be fused to all other forms of deliberation and discourse. Despite everything we've said in this chapter, not everyone's going to like it, but we're betting that most people will. It's adaptable, both in terms of the content to which it's applied and the process itself. It's now time to look closer at just what the IF approach involves and what it's trying to accomplish.

NOTES

1. Notice, we said "kind of person," not "person." They are what sociologists call "ideal types"—symbolic of the kinds of people who really exist. We wrote this chapter from the perspective of multiple ideal types rather than one or a couple of perspectives so that we could speak to many different kinds of people. Meanwhile, speaking to a variety of sometimes overlapping audiences as we do in this chapter is in keeping with the spirit that informs IF's work, an animus stressing multiple and contrasting possibilities. Finally, responding to this chapter's "ideal types" allows us to foreshadow some of the key features of IF's public discussions.

2. As Aristotle put it nearly two and a half millennia ago: "Leisure is a necessity, both for growth in goodness and for the pursuit of political activities" (*Politics*, 1329a). Sadly, leisure remains a scarce commodity, at least in the United States. Indeed, that the well-off participate disproportionately in American politics—and do so at a higher rate than the well off of perhaps any other developed country, is among political science's most robust findings. The classic work in the field: Verba, S., H. Nie, and J. Kim. 1978. *Participation and Political Equality.* Cambridge, England: Cambridge University Press.

3. Citing recent research in the field in online discussions, communications scholar Laura Black notes, "A relaxed sense of time can […] help participants feel less anxious about participating" in the face of work or family obligations." See Black, Laura. 2011. *The Promise and Problems of Online Deliberation.* Report prepared for the Charles F. Kettering Foundation, pp.12-13. The same can be said for IF's discussions. Lasting between four and six hours, they are long enough to create bonds between the participants but not too long as to be disruptive. Especially if the organizers take care of food, transportation, and child care, participants can really focus on the discussions, not what they're missing by attending them.

Let's Talk Politics

4. The same studies that document the skewed nature of political participation also tend to show that that participation is more skewed when it demands more money or time. (See the work cited in Note 2.) However, political discussion doesn't take a huge amount of time, requires little or no money, and can be quite energizing or "empowering."

5. It may be difficult to grasp what this might mean. But one answer follows from thinking about the various ways power is exercised. There is, of course, outright coercion, but power is also exercised when control is exerted over who gets to do the talking and what gets talked about. IF discussions very consciously seek to be as inclusive as possible. They invite participants to explore both the concerns that will frame their discussion, and possible responses to them.

6. Or, at least Bartlett's *Familiar Quotations* gives him the credit for doing so. See the Appendix of the 10th edition of 1919.

7. Charles W. Anderson places this view in the larger context of philosophical pragmatism's view of the state and society in *Pragmatic Liberalism*. 1990. Chicago, Ill.: University of Chicago Press. See especially Chaps. 3 and 12.

8. We describe these and other data at length in Chapter 4.

9. A need that the new information age may be disguising, as Neil Gabler, senior fellow at the Anenberg Norman Lear Center at the University of Southern California, points out. See "The Elusive Big Idea," *New York Times*. August 13, 2011. As communications scholars are finding out, the Web is good at creating "echo chambers" in which people find reinforcement for their ideas, less good at helping people respond to challenging ideas. (See the work cited in Note 3.)

10. We present evidence supporting this claim in Chapter 4. On the phenomenon of flaming more generally, see Black, Laura, 2011 (ibid.).

Let's Talk Politics

CHAPTER 4

— *Climbing the Stairway to Civility with Exploratory Discussions*

Come to an IF public discussion and you may be surprised at how it manages to combine passion and civility. That is no random result. It's the product of the many features of IF discussions working in concert, like various instruments in, say, a jazz band: lots of interplay but plenty of room for improvisation, too. Let's take a closer look. (If you're anxious to get directly to the results we've recorded in 200-plus IF public discussions, you can skip to the next chapter—though we'd strongly recommend giving this chapter at least a quick once-over.)[1]

CIVILITY AS A STAIRWAY

You've probably noticed that until now we've avoided a formal definition of "civility." We've done so consciously for two reasons: We didn't want anyone to seize upon a definition, disagree with it, and refuse to go any further in the book. The second reason for being intentionally "vague" is that we knew we'd need a chapter to explain what we mean by civility. This is that chapter.

Our thinking about "civility" begins with an appreciation for its complexity and richness. We deny that civility can be reduced to a single aim or destination, or even a collection of aims or destinations. Likewise, we can't bring ourselves to believe that civility is learned or acquired in a single way. Instead, our "definition"—or, more accurately, our model or theory—views civility as *an ascending sequence of interactive activities and goals*. This may seem straightforward, but there's more to this short phrase than meets the eye, so let's break it down.

First, our model stresses the notion that civility is a *sequence*, not a single thing or set of things. We see civility is a path, a course, and a direction.

Second, according to our model, the sequence is (or at least can be) *ascending*: there are stages or levels of civility—much like steps in a stairway. The first couple of chapters hinted at some of these, while the last chapter described each of them in no particular order. So let's lay them out now. The key steps in our model's sequence are: incivility, indifference, engaged commentary, conversational give-and-take, exploration of alternatives, co-exploration, and habituation. Each step represents higher or more advanced forms of civility.

Third, the model conceives of civility in terms of interactive activities and aims. This means, first and foremost, that each step up the stairway of civility will be more demanding in terms of skill and/or effort. This in turn means that each step up represents an achievement—and must be maintained through activity and practice.

To sum up what we've said so far, our theory views civility as a kind of never-ending path that requires actively and continually refining a set of skills. It is, in short, an explicitly developmental model,[3] which suggests a fourth feature: individual variation. Although we all fit on the stairway, each of us moves up and down as issues changes and as our individual circumstances vary. Likewise, because no two people are alike, everyone will experience opportunities to mount the stairway of civility in a unique way.

Finally, we return to the question of the interactions between aims and activities in our model of civility. Beyond saying that some need to be learned before others (like math, say, or like learning to play a new sport), our model specifies which sorts of activities are likely to promote which sorts of skills. It is, in that respect, a lot like the models educators come up with to figure out how best to promote learning outcomes in schools, agencies, groups, and firms.

This may all sound complicated, but it's easy enough to grasp with the help of a picture, which we provide below:

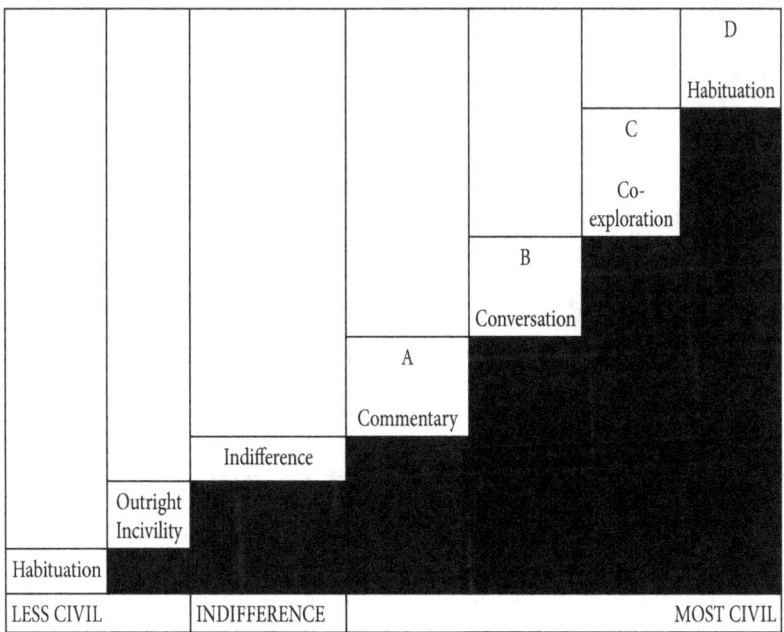

Figure 4.1. Stairway to Civility—A Developmental Model

In figure 4.1, the steps up the "stairway" are clearly labeled. Starting with step A, each indicates a skill, ability, or practice— one that, like a professional practice, must be continually used to be kept sharp. What Figure 4.1 doesn't indicate is *how* participants move up the stairway, that is, what it is about IF discussions that help them do so. Nor will we do so in this chapter except to highlight certain connections that we've already made in cataloguing the features of IF discussions in the last chapter. (These are the features that would fill in the area shaded in black in Figure 4.1.) Here, we would only add that each feature, from guidelines to facilitation, purpose to process, tends to encourage movement from the left to the right of Figure 4.1.[3]

This last point—that IF discussions encourage movement from *any* point on the stairway to a higher "step," may not sound remarkable, but it is—in two ways: First, because all facets of IF's public discussions promote each step up the stairway of civility—they tend to work no matter where a participant starts. IF discussions can take people as they find them regardless of their different starting points. Second, it means that IF discussions can offer something to everyone; everyone can get something positive from an IF discussion. This probably explains why we have accumulated so much positive evidence on the effect that they have had, which we detail in the next chapter. It is also best explains why IF discussions tend to be habit forming.[4]

Now let's take a closer look at the stairway, step by step.

STEP ONE—FROM INDIFFERENCE TO COMMENTARY

Participants in IF discussions tend not to be in-your-face hostile. In fact, coercion, bullying, and even more subtle forms of incivility are quite rare. So we'd like to begin by talking about what is a more typical "first step" for IF public discussion participants: the move from indifference to a lively exchange of opinions. Indifference is certainly preferable to outright incivility, but it can also be the result of bullying speech or behavior. For

Let's Talk Politics

a democracy to really thrive, citizens first have to be engaged. Exchanging opinions about a shared concern is a first step. It's also a precondition for what comes later as citizens move up the stairway of civility. If no one's talking at all, or no one's sticking to the subject at hand, then the more active sorts of interchange—what we call "interactivity"—demanded by the next step on the stairway cannot be taken.

The first significant step on the stairway of civility, from indifference to what we're calling "commentary," thus has three dimensions: participation, liveliness, and focus. All else being equal, the more involved everyone is the better. But involvement and energy alone don't make for commentary. For a collection of points to qualify as commentary, the comments have to converge around roughly the same concern, topic, or set of ideas. They have to be "about" the same thing—or at least moving in that direction. So the first question we look at in the next chapter is how do IF's public discussions measure up along the three dimensions of participation, energy, and focus? They measure up quite well. Indeed, the evidence is pretty overwhelming and indicates that the impact is significant.

While it is true that all of the features of IF's public discussions described in the last chapter contribute to each step up the stairway of civility, those that are especially important in engaging participants and keeping them "on topic" are a meal that breaks down barriers and encourages participants to see each other as people first, small groups that let everyone get in on the discussion, guidelines that encourage participation, a supportive environment, printed materials that focus the discussion, and facilitators who encourage participation and make sure it stays on point.

STEP TWO—FROM COMMENTARY TO CONVERSATION

Commentary, even if it stays on point, can involve little more than individual responses to the same event, question, or topic.

One need only to look at shows that gather "experts" together as examples. They succeed in eliciting relevant statements about the topic at hand but often fail to engage contributors. There is also nothing that guarantees that commentary amounts to anything more than emotional outbursts. To rise to the next level and make a more positive contribution to civility, commentary must take on another dimension: It must feature real exchanges between participants, which in turn requires that participants aren't simply echoing each others' thoughts but are instead taking different perspectives, suggesting distinctive points of view, and adding new insights. The next step up the stairway of civility, then, has two (mutually dependent) dimensions: a dynamic featuring authentic give-and-take and content featuring an exploration of alternatives. We use the label "conversation" for this step to distinguish it from "commentary" and because we think it does a good job of evoking an active, back-and-forth discussion about diverse ideas.

Our main measure of authentic exchange, or give-and-take, is the degree to which participants truly pay attention to what one another is saying. Following communications researchers, we sometimes call this "active listening." We also have several content measures that demonstrate the degree to which IF public discussions promote consideration of contrasting views. We have direct indicators that address participants' willingness to discuss contrasting concerns, possibilities, and consequences. We have indirect indicators measuring their tolerance for disagreement, and we ask how well the discussions avoided the kind of personal advocacy of a particular topic that can derail exploration.

It is in encouraging movement from a "bull session" to serious exploration that IF discussions really come into their own. Here, too, this is the result of many factors working together, but a few stand out as critical to helping participants make the step from commentary to conversation: the fellowship of a shared meal, IF's discussion materials (which provide an exploratory template by featuring alternatives), discussion guidelines that emphasize openness and are actively supported by a facilitator, and a process focused on contrasts.

STEP THREE—FROM CONVERSATION TO CO-EXPLORATION

The next step up the stairway of civility is what we call "co-exploration." In conversation, participants listen carefully to one another and react accordingly as they discuss alternatives. To conversation, co-exploration adds the idea of teamwork or working together.

"Working together" doesn't mean agreeing; it means exploring together, which participants can only do if they are willing to learn from one another. It can happen in a variety of ways: getting help in expressing an idea or building on a thought, working out the implications of a gut feeling or an instinct or a general sense, comparing notes, and so on.[5]

Learning from others doesn't necessarily involve "changing one's mind." It can be something less categorical though just as profound in its effects, including broadening one's understanding, gaining perspective, adding some nuance or detail—not to mention losing one's fear of those who have different ideas and instead seeing those ideas as indispensable to one's own growth. Get two conversationalists together and they will readily explore their disagreements, but get two co-explorers together, and they will help each other learn. In the process, they will appreciate each other more than the conversationalists. They will not only respect their differences, but they will also be grateful for them. This is a high level of civility, indeed.

Over time, we have tracked three basic quantitative measures of co-exploration. The first is the degree to which IF discussions encourage participants to value disagreement. The second is the degree to which they prompt participants to actively add to each others' ideas during discussions. The third, and possibly most intriguing, is the degree to which they lead to learning and how participants describe it. Again, the evidence we have accumulated so far is quite positive.

As with Steps 1 and 2, all aspects of IF discussions have some role to play in helping participants take the step from conversation to co-exploration. Team-building begins with a shared meal, which encourages participants to treat each other first as neighbors or co-citizens. Later the discussion is formalized and protected by the guidelines. Finally, it is nurtured by the facilitator. Keeping contrasts firmly at the center of discussions is the key to keeping them exploratory.

STEP FOUR—FROM OCCASIONAL CO-EXPLORATION TO CO-EXPLORATION AS A HABIT

You may have noticed in looking at Figure 4.1 that "habituation" appears at both the bottom and top of the stairway to civility. That reflects our view that if civility doesn't become ingrained, there is a natural tendency for people to backslide down the stairway. When repeated practice in the right kind of activities become a habit, one has arrived at the top "rung" of the ladder of civility.

We consider habituation to civility-as-co-exploration a higher step than co-exploration. Repetition is what makes for a good habit, as opposed to a one-time thing. It's what turns civility into routine.

We have several indicators of habituation. They are robust, because they involve triangulation. They are indirect, because they have to do with how much participants *value* IF discussions rather than whether they are actually engaging in regular "co-exploration." The three measures are: willingness to participate in another IF discussion, actual repeat participation (obviously a more solid measure, though somewhat more difficult to interpret), and willingness to engage in IF-style discussions with other people. We think it's safe to assume that if people are regularizing their discussion experience, they are also doing more and more co-exploration, since we have seen that same pattern regularly develop over the course of individual IF discussion series. If participants tend to co-explore more in session three than they did in session one, in other words, it seems reasonable to expect that they will co-explore more in discussion series three than they did in discussion series one.

Disentangling how the various features of IF discussions combine to support habituation would be even more difficult, we suspect, than for the other steps up the ladder of civility. Almost certainly, every one contributes something. Still, when asked what they most appreciated about IF's public discussions, participants tend to mention some combination of exploration and civility. To the extent that this is true, it further confirms our view that exploration promotes civility. It also confirms the idea that civility begets civility—that civility is habit forming.

NARROWING IMPACT SHOWS INCREASING DIFFICULTY OF EACH STEP

As the next chapter will show, we have very encouraging evidence about the impact of IF's public discussion at each step up the stairway of civility. But the evidence weakens as we go up. It is strongest at the lowest step. Our evidence about the move from "commentary to conversation" is not as strong as the evidence we have about IF discussions' ability to encourage movement from indifference to commentary. As we'll see at each step of the way, the evidence, although convincing, indicates a drop off in IF public discussions' impacts in the sense that they tend to impact fewer and fewer people. This might suggest that our discussions are flawed, but we strongly believe that such an interpretation would be off the mark. Instead, we think it is more appropriate, given the abundance of evidence we will present in the next chapter, to see the drop off as confirmation of the interaction between two key features of our model, namely that each step is more difficult than the last and that there is a great amount of individual variation among participants. Since it becomes harder to take each additional step, and since different people have different abilities and opportunities, it stands to reason that fewer will benefit at each step up the stairway.

But enough about the model. It's time to get to that evidence.

NOTES

1. The reason this chapter is worth a quick read is that its theoretical model not only ties together what we said about the multiple individual elements of IF public discussions in Chapter 2 but is also the source of the measures that we report on in the next chapter, where we describe evidence supporting the value of IF public discussions. The evidence there strongly suggests that IF discussions have been a success. The model presented in this chapter thus both explains what we *mean* by "success" and describes the various measures we used to assess it.

2. Some readers might detect echoes of Piaget and Kohlberg here—but they are not as strong as they might seem. Our model, while developmental, differs from those of these well-known figures in several ways. To name just a few: it is limited in scope to civility rather than encompassing cognition or moral reasoning *toute courte*; it admits multiple forms of intelligence on an equal footing with cognition; it treats opportunity and effort as variables of importance equal to that of innate development; and, consequently, it conceives of development as always partial, always subject to backsliding.

3. This last difference merits special emphasis: civility is developmental both in the short term (over the course of a discussion, say) and long term (over the course of a lifetime). Here and in the next chapter we discuss measures and

evidence pertaining principally to the former. Our intention is to expand our research to measure the longer-term impacts of IF discussions as well.

4. We do not attempt in this book to sort out the *level* or *degree* of influence of the many different aspects of IF discussions. Neither do we try to distill the reciprocal impact of civility on the various features of IF public discussions. Both tasks must await further research. We note only that sorting these influences out is well worth attempting by anyone interested in fine-tuning the IF approach.

5. It's also worth keeping in mind that IF discussions have a positive impact on civility not because they explicitly aim to make participants "more civil," invite them to "chill out" or try to make them "less hostile." IF discussions work by encouraging exploration, and it is the activity of exploratory discussion that encourages civility. For more on the objectives of IF discussions, see Adolf G. Gundersen, "Public Discussion as the Exploration and Development of Contrasting Conceptual Possibilities," published by the Interactivity Foundation, Parkersburg, West Virginia, November 2006: http://www.interactivityfoundation.org/resources-downloads/papers (particularly the essays making up section U).

6. Of course, it can also happen when simply taking a difference of opinion seriously, but we consider this an aspect of conversation.

CHAPTER 5

— A Proven Track Record

This chapter reviews IF's track record in moving citizens up the "ladder of civility." We think we have plenty of reasons to be proud of the record we—and our participants—have established. It shows that we are making real progress as a Foundation in promoting our mission of enhancing democratic discussion and the civility that results from it. We hope you'll decide to be part of it.

This chapter is divided into four main sections. Each section corresponds to one of the steps on the "ladder of civility" described in Chapter 4. (Note that each section describes not one but *multiple* measures or indicators of the movements described in Chapter 4's model. Keep in mind, too, that we are reporting on more than 1,000 responses from facilitators and participants alike, responses that include both open-ended and closed questions.) We begin with the lowest step, presenting measures of and evidence for movement from indifference to active engagement, and we conclude with a description of indicators of movement from constructive discussion to habituation. As you will see, the evidence is uniformly positive for every measure at every step of the ladder. This is what gives us confidence that you can share in our success if you put your mind to it and follow the guidelines we offer in Chapters 6-8.[1]

EVIDENCE OF MOVEMENT FROM INDIFFERENCE TO COMMENTARY

Chapter 4 explains that the first step up the ladder of civility is from indifference to commentary. A number of measures combine to indicate how clear and prevalent this movement has been in IF discussions: several relating to participation levels, others to the liveliness of the discussions, and an indirect indicator of how focused the discussions have been.[2] Together, they indicate that IF discussions help participants make the move from relative passivity to active exchange with others.

Participation

Just over half of our participants tell us that compared with past policy discussions they felt "much freer" or "freer" to contribute during their IF discussion. More tellingly, nearly 60% of our participants report being more willing to contribute to the discussion as it went on. An almost identical number of facilitators (61%) say the same is true of shy participants.

Liveliness

IF has employed dozens of facilitators over the past five years. They are nearly unanimous in reporting that their IF discussions are the most lively they have ever experienced. We ask facilitators whether the possibilities covered in the reports they use during their discussions "stimulated discussion." The range that said they "agree" or "strongly agree" ranges from 76% to more than 95%—falling off only after participants have discussed six possibilities, which usually marks the end of our discussions.[3]

Focus

Participation, even lively participation, doesn't count for much unless it is relevant. We know from our qualitative analysis of open-ended questions that one of the main challenges facilitators face is keeping lively discussions focused on exploration.[3] We have no direct indicator of their success in meeting this challenge. However, we have two indirect measures of the focused nature of IF discussions: Two-thirds of our participants agreed with the statement, "As a result of the discussion, I am more likely to think about the area of concern." A nearly identical number agreed with the statement, "As a result of the discussion, I am more likely to pay attention to media stories about the area of concern."

EVIDENCE OF MOVEMENT FROM COMMENTARY TO CONVERSATION

As participants become more engaged, the expectation from the model developed in Chapter 4 is that they will move from commentary to conversation. This involves acquiring—or reinforcing—the habit of active listening, which means not just hearing others out, but concentrating on what they say—and then really processing it. We focused our questions on the simpler question of whether IF discussions help people overcome barriers to more active processing. Because this was such an important question, we asked it in two ways: Do IF discussions lead people to be more tolerant of disagreement? Do they lead people to consider a wider range of perspectives? Our evidence is based on more than 150 facilitator responses and more than 850 participant responses. It indicates that IF discussions do indeed have all of these effects.

Active Listening

Just over 41% of our participants agreed with the statement, "As the discussion wore on, I listened more and talked less"; roughly one-eighth of that group strongly agreed. Only 13% of our participants disagreed or strongly disagreed with it. This is admittedly not an overly revealing finding since we did not directly query participants as to whether they found themselves listening *more actively* as the discussions progressed, only whether they listened more or less. More direct evidence comes from our facilitators, more than 79% of whom agreed that "as the discussion went along, participants listened more carefully to one another" (nearly one-third of them strongly). Given these findings, we find little reason to doubt that IF discussions promote active listening.

Tolerating Disagreement

Participants generally responded to open-ended questions about disagreement by simply acknowledging that it existed, rather than saying that they choose to actively engage them. Nevertheless, when asked directly to describe the role of disagreement in IF discussions, participants generally admitted it was valuable. For some, this was because differences in point of view deepened or altered their own thinking; for others, it was because such differences led them to appreciate, in the words of one participant, that "each of us forms our conclusions based on our respective experiences and that those vary widely."

Considering Alternative Perspectives

Ninety percent of our participants *and* facilitators agreed with the statement that IF discussions encourage participants to consider alternative points of view. (Of the participant group, more than half strongly agreed; of the facilitator group, more than one-third strongly agreed). The vast majority of our participants also report that their discussion encouraged them to consider a wide range of concerns, policy possibilities, and policy consequences, as the following graph shows.[4]

Figure 5.1. Impact of Discussion upon Participants' Consideration of Other Viewpoints.

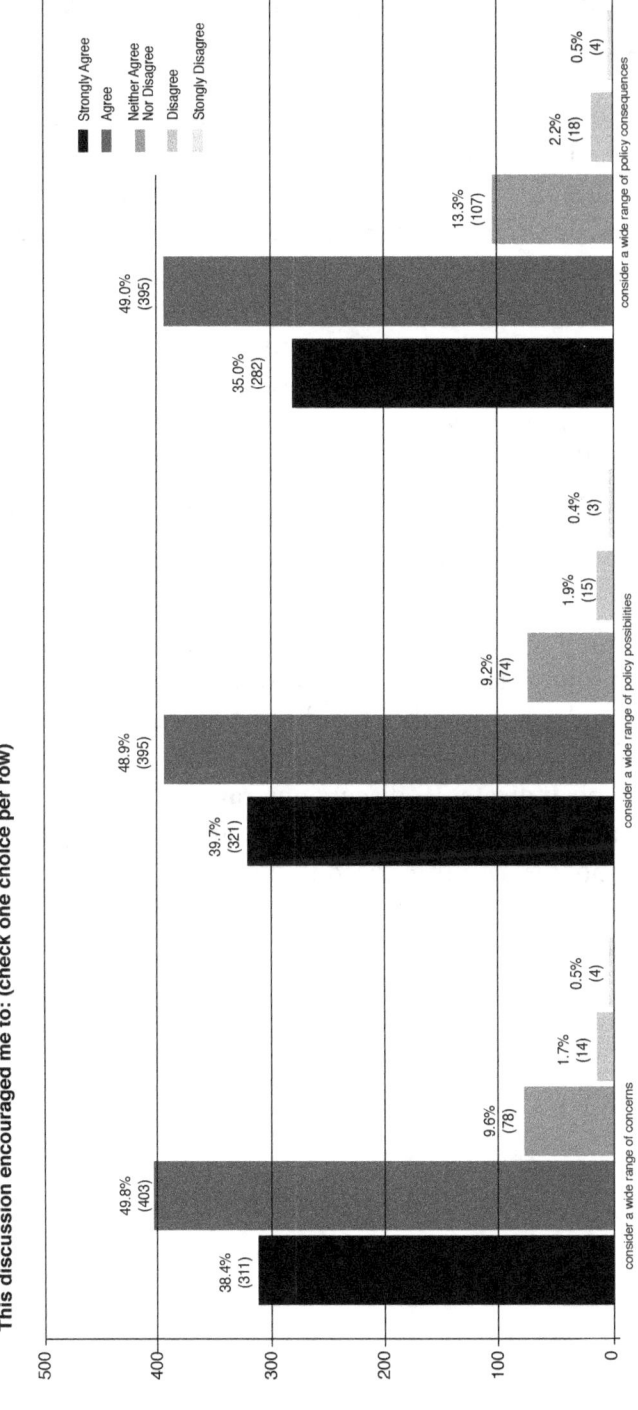

EVIDENCE OF MOVEMENT FROM CONVERSATION TO CO-EXPLORATION

The next step up the model developed in Chapter 4 is from conversation to co-exploration. This involves actively adding something new to one's own ideas and/or to those of other participants. On the last several pages, we presented evidence that IF discussions lead participants' to consider alternative perspectives, evidence that might also be interpreted as a measure of the degree to which participants expand their thinking during IF discussions. But merely *considering* others' perspectives is not the same as *building* on them. Fortunately, we have evidence from both our closed and open-ended questions that not only document this change, but suggest why it occurs.

Building on Other's Ideas

Our first indicator that IF discussions encourage participants to build on others' ideas comes from responses to a question that simply asks whether the discussion changed participants' views and, if so, how. As the results summarized in the following graph indicate, IF discussions rarely change *what* people think about a topic—but they very often do change *how* they think about it, as summarized in the following graph:

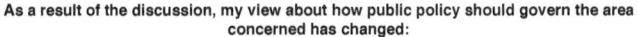

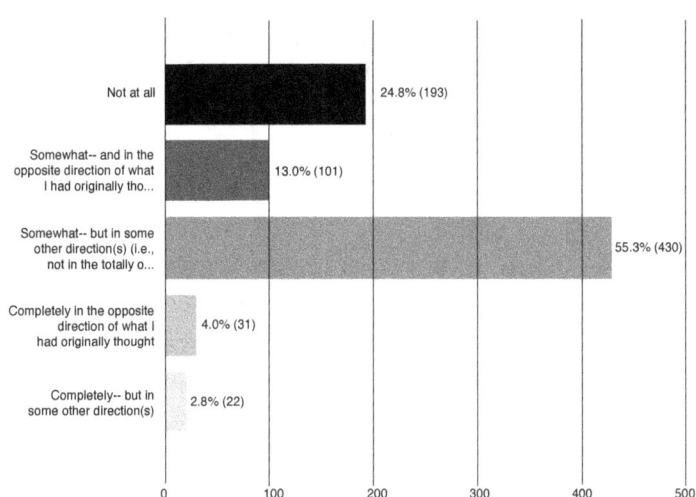

Figure 5.2. Impact of Discussion upon Participants' Attitudes Towards Governance of Area of Concern.

Of the 61% of participants who answered this question, approximately six out of seven said that, as a result of the discussion, their views had "changed somewhat—and mostly in a different (but not necessarily opposite) direction."

Additional qualitative analysis has allowed us to delve deeper into this general description. What it has revealed is that *by far and away the largest majority of participant responses to open-ended questions regarding the effect of our public discussions has dealt with understanding other perspectives more or differently.* Either participants volunteered that they learned about ideas they had not previously explored or came to reconsider previously held beliefs, in the process opening themselves to new ideas, positions, and people, toward whom they were previously indifferent or even hostile. Because these responses were not prompted by any specific language on our part, we think they are a robust indicator of how participants move from active processing to co-exploration.

We also can offer a clear explanation for how this movement occurs—an explanation that goes beyond participants' consideration of alternatives. Large majorities of participants report that IF discussions encourage them to think about public policy *conceptually* and in terms of *possibilities* (77% and 85%, respectively)—that is, to think in terms of what might be rather than what is or what must or should be. To use Shakespeare's term, IF discussions encourage participants to think in terms of "ifs." It would be hard to underestimate the significance of this finding, because it directly links IF's exploratory discussion approach to participants' movement from active engagement to co-exploration. Shakespeare may have been exaggerating when he observed that "your if is the only peacemaker," but this finding strongly confirms our belief that discussing possibilities rather than choices, set positions, or fixed beliefs paves the way for individual learning.

EVIDENCE OF MOVEMENT FROM CO-EXPLORATION TO HABITUATION

The final step up the ladder of civility is from co-exploration to habituation, from engaging in exploratory discussion on a one-off basis to making it a part of one's civic habits. This is a big step, to be sure. When practitioners and social scientists engage citizens in discussion or "deliberation," the most they typically hope for is that citizens will apply the experience to a single act—such as an upcoming election. The notion that discussion can have a *lasting* impact is almost unheard of. Yet we see it all the time. Our experience is that IF discussions heighten participants' willingness to participate in additional discussions, seek them out (whether sponsored by IF or not), and even alter civic habits that involve "more" than talk.[5]

Willingness to Participate in Additional IF Discussions

Slightly more than half (59%) of our participants report that they would "definitely" participate in another IF discussion; another 25% say they would "probably" do so. (Fewer than one in 50 tell us that they would "definitely not" participate again.)

Discussion With Others

That our participants want to keep working with us is gratifying. Far more gratifying, however, is the capacity of the IF process to promote dialogue even after our discussions are over. That IF discussions can promote *further* dialogue after we "leave the scene" constitutes even stronger evidence than repeat participation in IF discussions of the movement from co-exploration to habituation to discussion.[6]

Our research shows that IF discussions encourage participants to keep talking about public policy both about the specific area covered during the discussion and about other policy areas. Nearly two-thirds of our participants (65%) report being more likely to discuss the topic of their IF discussion with other people after participating in one of our discussions. Willingness to participate in additional discussion groups did not decline when IF's name was omitted from the question: more than 87% agreed with the statement that "participating in this discussion series makes it much more likely that I will participate in another citizen discussion" (more than half of this group agreed strongly). More remarkable still is that almost half of our participants (47%) say that their IF discussion resulted in their being more likely to encourage *others* (family, friends, and neighbors) to discuss the topic they covered in their IF discussion. This ripple effect even extends to participants' declared willingness to discuss public policy more generally: More than one-third (38%) tell us that their discussion led them to be more likely to discuss other public policies.

IF discussions reportedly encourage participants to engage in a wide range of political activities, as the following graph shows:

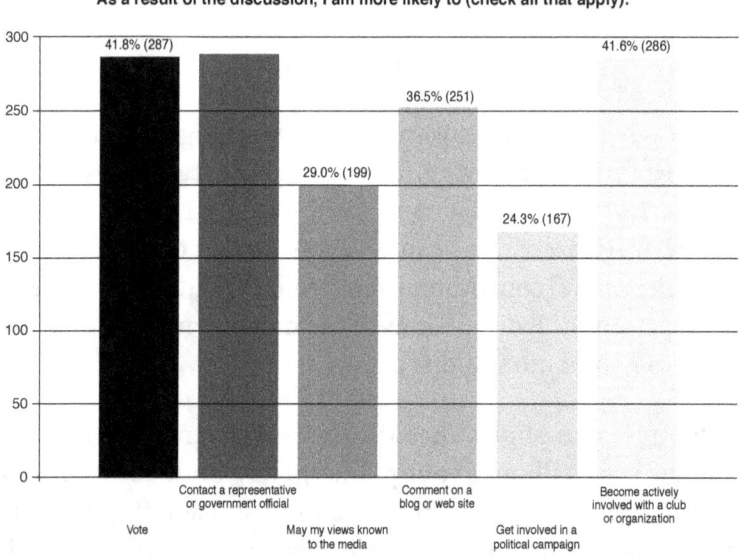

As a result of the discussion, I am more likely to (check all that apply):

Figure 5.3. Impact of Discussion upon Participants' Political Engagement.

Although it is true that the gains indicated above are not evenly spread, their range and frequency is impressive.[7] Indeed, one would have to search high and low in the literature on democratic discussion to find anything that comes close. Most social scientists and practitioners are pleased when they can discern the impact of discussion on what or how people think, something we've documented in our own discussions above. Very few have observed real impacts on single political actions, such as referendum or electoral votes. A handful have shown that citizens can meaningfully engage in real-world deliberative processes, but what our evidence illuminates is something much more profound: a discursive dynamic that first takes hold during a single discussion, then is carried beyond it, and finally is connected to action on a habitual basis.

NOTES

1. We think scholars will be interested and more than a bit surprised by our findings—especially those that indicate lasting impacts on participants' civic habits (as opposed to individual decisions or actions), findings which have no parallel in the wide literature on democratic deliberation that we know of. Indeed, they might even be skeptical of our sampling or analytical methods. Since this is a practical rather than scholarly work, we offer no lengthy defense of either here. We believe our mixed sample, described in Appendix II, understates the gains in civility we describe in this chapter. And we would remind any who might be suspicious of our analytical approach that we limit ourselves here to simple tabulations, supported occasionally by conventional computer-supported qualitative analysis. We aim soon to elaborate on both our sampling and analytical methods in a future monograph.

2. That IF participants find our discussions stimulating is also indirectly evidenced by high levels of repeat performance and expressed willingness to participate in additional IF discussions. Since these are also direct indicators of habituation to discussion, they are described in the last section of the chapter.

3. Maintaining energy and focus at the same time is a challenge, as any seasoned facilitator can tell you. The more excited participants get, the more they tend to stray from the task at hand—in this case exploring concerns and possibilities for addressing them. For this reason, it makes sense to consider these findings as a cluster.

4. Similar but even higher numbers were reported by facilitators, ranging from 88% agreement for "consequences" to 96% for "concerns."

5. These outcomes might also act as explanatory "pathways" to other gains in civility, particularly gains in tolerance. We are indebted to our research assistant Anna Wiederhold for suggesting this hypothesis, which we hope to test soon.

6. It also shows that as a Foundation, we are making headway in broadening democratic discussion. We aim to gauge this progress more accurately in the future.

7. Although higher educated participants (those with a college and/or graduate degree) were slightly more likely to report reading more media stories about the area of concern explored in their discussion than those with less education, the other gains reported in this subsection were even more pronounced among participants with less education.

CHAPTER 6

— How to Prepare for an IF-Style Public Discussion

If you're reading this chapter, it's safe to assume you are ready to experiment with an IF discussion of your own. We are ready to help get you started. Keep in mind that our advice is thoroughly grounded in careful analysis of the feedback we have received from both participants and facilitators in the 250-plus discussions IF facilitators have conducted over the past five years.[1]

The first thing to understand is that with IF discussions, the right kind of preparation goes a long way toward maximizing your chances of success and amplifying the success you do have. So that's where we begin in this chapter. As a review and to help keep you organized, we've included a "To-Do" checklist on pages 99-100.

THE BASICS

Let's start with the basics: *The main tasks you'll need to complete in preparation for four to eight hours of IF-style exploratory discussion are to get together a small group of participants and a facilitator and arrange for a meal and in-depth exploratory discussion in a comfortable setting. The task of getting people together requires both being ready to explain the purpose of IF's discussions and scheduling.*[2] (We'll deal with the ins and outs of *conducting* an IF discussion in the following chapter.)

WHO—Finding a Facilitator and Participants

First, you'll need to find an able facilitator, or someone willing to get training. Look for someone who's got good leadership skills and is also a good listener. He or she needs to keep the discussion "under control" (on topic) but also keep it moving in an exploratory way, which requires careful attention to everything everyone says along the way. The more experienced your facilitator is, the faster he or she is likely to pick up on what's involved in IF discussions. And, as with anything else, practice makes for improvement.

You'll also need to find a small group of willing participants. We recommend eight as the ideal number. Six works best in actual discussion, we've found; recruiting a few extras allows for absences. As we said in Chapter 2, a group of five to eight will be big enough for a variety of viewpoints, but small enough that everyone will have a chance to talk, get to know one another, and feel less pressure to either conform or persuade others to. We do not recommend that you have more than 10 participants.

As for the right type and mix of participants, keep in mind that you're not looking for experts or policy professionals, but simply interested citizens. Anyone who *wants* to participate is at least minimally qualified to participate. We've held successful discussions with a variety of participants. The discussions, as we've seen, will tend to improve everyone's exploratory abilities. Still, you'll have to use your own best judgment about the degree to which your facilitator will be able to manage problems such as distrust, bossiness, and outright hostility. Meanwhile, it can be helpful to the facilitator to "seed" the discussion group with a couple of participants who can be counted on to contribute

Let's Talk Politics

alternative perspectives or, better still, engage in co-exploration of the topic at hand (i.e., who will help others develop their thoughts).[3] Finally, our research shows that it is helpful to know your audience, especially their degree of familiarity with the topic. If they are uncertain about a particular topic, be ready to spend more time on the report's introductory sections; some groups may appreciate having additional background information to provide context for the discussion.

Getting people together for an IF discussion is not difficult as long as you rely on people or groups you're connected with to spread the word or on groups that already have an interest in discussing public affairs. If someone you're recruiting has "pull," they may help you recruit. They may lead others to join them in the discussion—or persuade them to. As long as all of your participants aren't of a single mind on the concern you'll be discussing, it shouldn't be too hard to keep them from engaging in "group think." In return, your contacts will help make the task of putting a discussion group together easier and faster.[4]

Although we recommend the "direct" approach to recruiting for public discussions, there are others that can work, too, either alone or in combination. Online tools, in particular, are useful, offering the advantages of efficiency and reach. Social media, e-mail, and "listservs" all make it easier to reach a wide and varied pool of potential participants. They also make it easier to be selective about whom you will involve. Finally, they can make scheduling a snap (though be sure to "over-recruit" if you use an electronic approach because it is easier for would-be participants to forget about a meeting or to decide at the last minute not to show).

WHY—The Purpose of IF Public Discussions

It's nearly impossible to get people together for anything without making it clear what's in it for them. People will naturally want to know why they should come to an IF discussion. Our research shows that clearly explaining the benefits of participating in an IF public discussion is crucial, not only during recruiting, but also during and after the discussion itself. Customize your elevator speech in two ways: First, make it your own, so that it feels natural. Second, recognize each participant as an individual. Everyone is different and will find the discussions valuable for different reasons. However, the key elements come down to this: IF discussions are an opportunity to socialize, build relationships, and get involved in the democratic process in a way that encourages active learning about public policy and builds civic skills. Plus, they're fun.[5]

WHEN—Scheduling

IF discussions can last anywhere from four to fourteen hours, depending on the participants' interest level. Keep your schedule flexible, but count on two or three three-hour sessions, including time for a meal. Our feedback also shows that participants appreciate breaks to re-energize and have more informal talks; schedule them in. Exploration—and the social dynamics that underlie and result from it—takes time. All-day events make it easier for everyone to keep track of the conversation, but they are taxing and difficult to fit in for most people. One session per week seems to work best because that minimizes gaps in the discussion. Given the number of people involved, scheduling can tricky even with shorter sessions. You can either "recruit to a (fixed) schedule," which tends to be the simplest, or ask people when they can make it and sort out dates later. Either way, it's helpful to print up a schedule of the agenda so that everyone has a reminder of when and where you'll be meeting, as well as the order of events (more on that in the next chapter).

WHAT—Choosing Content

The easiest way to have an IF-style discussion is to focus on an existing IF discussion report, because they are designed to keep your group focused on exploratory discussion.[6] (You'll find an annotated list of current and planned topics at the end of this chapter on pages 88-89.) As organizer, you can choose the topic yourself or have your group make the choice. Either way, you'll need to order enough copies for everyone: participants and facilitator. Our research shows that it is best to distribute these a week or two before the discussion, which gives participants time to read and reflect, yet it's not too far in advance that people forget the topic of discussion. It is fine to distribute the report at the first meeting, too. (Our experience is that many people don't have time to read the report very carefully before the first meeting, and it is best not to make people feel as if they *must* read it in advance. After all, this is a discussion group, not a study group.) However, our participants and facilitators have made it clear that the more familiar the facilitator is with the report ahead of time, the better. Familiarizing yourself with the material helps you think about relevant follow-up questions ahead of time and to conduct the session once it gets going.

WHERE—Choosing a Venue

IF discussions can take place in any private or semi-private space, from picnic grounds to your neighborhood school's gym or cafeteria. When choosing a place to hold your discussion, remember that you'll want to include a meal and make sure that the venue is easy for everyone to get to. It should also be quiet and well lit. Participants tell us that they appreciate having free and accessible parking—even better if your venue is accessible via public transportation. Often the best choice is a potluck in someone's living room, which reduces costs, highlights the notion of sharing, and makes child care easier to arrange.

If you decide to meet at a restaurant, remember to ask for a quiet space (a corner section or a private room). In order to minimize interruptions during the meal, you might try to work with the restaurant to limit menu options. Getting participants' menu requests in advance via e-mail also helps make it easier to manage the meal. Spacing sections of your discussion between appetizers, entrees, and desserts can also help to pace your discussion.

Seating is important, too. Input from past participants and facilitators tells us that round tables work best because they allow everyone to be seen and heard. Chinese restaurants tend to have big round tables that encourage discussion and allow for ready sharing of food. Many of our discussion groups have incorporated a "moms' night out" approach, or even an afternoon "playgroup" motif. Stay-at-home moms (and dads) are, we've found, ideal participants since they enjoy the opportunity to discuss politics and policy ideas. A playgroup setting allows for more readily available child care. Libraries, religious institutions, and community centers also work well and may already have programs in place that facilitate child care or potlucks. It is important to think through logistics, such as child care, transportation, and meals, ahead of time with an eye to keeping costs low and participation as broad as possible. You'll find that coming up with ways of including a broader array of participants in your discussions is easier than you think. There's no one way to overcome the challenges that might prevent people from participating. Be creative.

BEFORE THE DISCUSSION STARTS—A CHECKLIST

Don't sweat the details. Once you've got the people, place, and food scheduled, and discussion materials on order, you'll be set. Remember, if people accept your invitation, it's because they want to be there. Talking is natural.

- ▶ PEOPLE
  - ◊ Facilitator
    - Scheduled
    - Contact information recorded
  - ◊ 8-10 participants
    - Scheduled
    - Contact information recorded
- ▶ TIMETABLE, Scheduled
- ▶ PLACE, scheduled
- ▶ FOOD, scheduled
- ▶ (CHILD CARE, arranged)
- ▶ DISCUSSION MATERIALS
  - ◊ Discussion guidelines
  - ◊ Discussion agenda
  - ◊ Discussion Report
    - Ordered
    - Reviewed by facilitator
    - Distributed to participants
  - ◊ List of other discussion topics

A LIST OF RESOURCES

Discussion Reports: Available at no cost in printed form directly from IF (mail request to P.O. Box 9; Parkersburg, West Virginia; 26102-0009). Also downloadable directly from the IF Website (see next entry).

▶ New titles to the IF catalogue of discussion reports are constantly being added, and old titles are updated regularly. Titles that are now available include:

▶ Anticipating Human Genetic Technology

▶ Climate Change

▶ Crime & Punishment

▶ Democratic Nation Building

▶ Energy

▶ Food: What Might Be for Dinner?

▶ The Future of the Arts in a Democratic Society

▶ The Future of Childhood

▶ The Future of the Family

▶ The Future of K-12 Education

▶ Future Possibilities for Civil Rights Policy

▶ Helping America Talk

▶ Helping Out

▶ How Will We All Retire?

- Higher Education

- Human Migration

- Medical Care: The Case of Depression

- Money, Credit, and Debt

- Privacy

- The Promise of American Democracy

- Property

- Public Policy and Shaping America's Towns and Cities

- Science

For a description of any of these reports and the projects that produced them, or for the most up-to-date version of this list, consult the IF Website www.interactivityfoundation.org.

Website of the Interactivity Foundation: www.interactivity-foundation.org

This resource is the single best way to access all materials you might want to consult as you plan this phase of the discussion.

Facilitation Guidebook for Small Group Public Discussions: Contains tips on all aspects of planning and conducting pubic discussions. Available at no cost in printed form directly from IF (order through IF Website, above, or mail request to P.O. Box 9; Parkersburg, West Virginia; 26102-0009). Also downloadable directly from the IF Website, listed above.

Perspectives on Public Discussion: Background material in the form of postings from IF Fellows and collaborators on doing IF-style discussions. Downloadable directly from the IF Website, listed above.

NOTES

1. Feedback included more than 1,000 responses to both open-ended and closed questions. Both quantitative and qualitative analysis continues on this data. Here in this book, we report only our preliminary results. We aim to follow up this practical book with one describing our research methods and results in much more detail.

2. Although we focus on small-group, in-person discussions here, most of what we say in this chapter and in the rest of the book applies to online discussions, as well. It is important to keep in mind, however, that online discussions lack the good will that is naturally generated from face-to-face interaction, particularly when such fellowship occurs over a shared meal. This can make an online facilitator's job harder, as uncivil flare-ups can thus occur more readily.

3. Remember that you're looking for diversity of viewpoints, not demographic diversity. Even if it were possible to achieve demographic diversity within a small group, "representativeness" might backfire if anyone feels as if they are being considered the spokesperson of a particular interest group rather than a "co-explorer." Also, it can be common for people of a shared social class status to have little diversity in terms of experiences and perspectives, even if the group is diverse with regard to race or ethnicity. To find a wide representation of viewpoints, do your best to look within your existing social circles and surroundings. Both authors have used PTAs, rotary clubs, athletic activities, churches, and other venues to find participants. Meetup.org is also a good forum for finding a nice array of people who are interested in discussion—though you will have little sense of these individuals and their discussion styles before you meet them. IF discussions have also been well-received within places that seek discursive activities, such as retirement centers and at-risk youth intervention programs. Try

to think in terms of putting together groups in which the participants might not normally sit down and talk with one another.

4. Thanks to Dennis Boyer and James L. Schneider for the pointers described in this paragraph.

5. For more on the purposes, aims, and objectives of IF discussions, see Adolf G. Gundersen, *Public Discussion as the Exploration and Development of Contrasting Conceptual Possibilities,* published by the Interactivity Foundation, Parkersburg, West Virginia, November 2006: http://www. interactivityfoundation.org/resources-downloads/papers (particularly the essays making up section U).

6. It would be possible, of course, to conduct an IF-style exploratory discussion about almost anything that interested you. In that case, our existing Reports might be useful models whose format you could alter as you went along.

CHAPTER 7

— How to Conduct an IF-Style Public Discussion

Conducting a successful IF discussion is a lot like redirecting a stream of water into new areas. It requires two things: enforcing limits, or what we've been calling "guidelines" (to keep the water from overflowing its banks), and encouraging exploration (to channel the water into places it hasn't been before). The kind of engineering required to get this done may sound pretty daunting, but it's far from rocket science. Like any stream, your participants won't need any encouragement to "flow"; they'll do that naturally. What you'll need to do is to make sure that their flow is *exploratory*. Accomplishing that is a skill, and it improves with experience. If you can maintain some order and spur people to try on new ways of thinking, you can do it. Read on and we think you'll agree.

THE BASICS

If you've done a reasonably good job of planning, conducting your IF public discussion will come down to keeping participants exploring alternatives and doing so at a conceptual or general level. If everyone's flashlight stays on, scanning the middle distance, you'll make good progress. The biggest challenge

IF facilitators tend to face is preventing any single participant from dominating the discussion, as so often happens in casual conversation. In fact, *the single biggest lesson we've learned from our research on IF public discussions is that facilitators need to be assertive.* It can be difficult to tread the fine line of allowing participants freedom to speak and maintaining the flow of the conversation, but nearly 75% of our facilitators and more than 90% of our participants have recommended firmer intervention to deal with dominant personalities, so don't be afraid to facilitate assertively. Here are some specific recommendations culled from our research on how to do this:

- ▶ Sit next to dominant speakers

- ▶ Encourage quieter participants to speak up

- ▶ Keep to the timetable

- ▶ Excuse disruptive persons

- ▶ Take fewer notes

As facilitator, you can't let anyone turn your discussion into a monologue or lecture, no matter how interesting or authoritative. This can be tricky, because you want to make everyone feel included. Just remember this rule, which covers both sides of that coin: *Once the discussion gets underway, the facilitator's number one responsibility is to make sure that the discussion remains a discussion.* Following this rule—by direct intervention to provide air time to quieter participants and draw them out, if necessary, perhaps reinforced with carefully worded one-on-one reminders during breaks—will give everyone a chance to speak and to listen. With everyone chiming in, the group will quickly evolve into a team, and even the biggest loudmouth will come to see that exploring ideas with others is more rewarding than "telling them where it's at."

LEVEL

Remember that IF public discussions are intended to be pitched at what we call a "conceptual level": the sweet spot between airy abstractions and technical detail. This feature of IF discussions is important not just because it tends to be ignored in conventional political discussion, but also because it evens the playing field between "experts" and lay citizens. By example, IF Reports will help you and your participants keep the discussion at the conceptual level by providing contrasting policy possibilities, examples and consequences of various policy approaches, and discussion questions. The reports are designed to present an array of politically contrasting possibilities so as to include the widest range of perspectives. As facilitator, you may well have to remind participants to stick to the discussion rules, avoid advocacy, and remain at a conceptual level with the discussion, as our experience shows that some people are inclined to talk a lot about particular cases they know well or argue rather than explore a wider range of ideas and perspectives.

SEQUENCE

The various steps to be followed in an IF discussion tend to unfold naturally: criss-crossing and circling back, racing ahead, and going off on tangents. Yet no two discussions are alike, although the logical structure of an IF discussion is easy to sketch out. It's useful to have this sketch in mind, however much you end up deviating from it during an actual discussion.

Step 1. Personal introductions. IF discussion participants spend a significant amount of time together, sometimes discussing sensitive issues. Our research is clear on this point: Don't try to jump into your discussion too quickly; allow time for people to get to know one another or renew old acquaintances, preferably over a meal.

Step 2. Introduction to IF, exploratory discussion, and the Report. It's a good bet that some or most of your participants won't know much, if anything, about IF or "exploratory discussion." Take a moment at the start of the discussion to determine whether participants want to learn more about the Foundation or its process by discussing the introductory materials in the Report. This is also the time to outline how the discussion will be run and to let participants know that it will include an opportunity for both oral and written feedback. Make sure that everyone is comfortable with the purpose and the process. Participants tell us facilitators can't be clear enough on these points.

Step 3. Agreement on Discussion Guidelines. You can move easily from talking about the IF process to getting agreement on discussion guidelines. Here, too, participants speak with nearly one voice: Clarity about the rules of road are one of the most important ingredients to the success of an IF discussion. Once you have it, you're ready to go.

Step 4. Discussion of Participants' Concerns Regarding Topic. Although some groups like talking about the IF process, which can help build trust and understanding, your participants will likely want to move through the preliminaries quickly. They came together to talk about public policy, so let them. Leave the IF Report to the side for a while and start with what brought them to the discussion: their interests, their perspectives, their concerns. We've found that exploring participants' own concerns at the outset is an especially effective way to:

▶ generate immediate interest and involvement in the discussion, because people are most comfortable when they start by talking about their own interest in a subject. (Participants will often come back after the first session talking about things they heard in the news or talked about with friends.)

- ▶ help participants understand the conceptual possibilities presented in the discussion Report

- ▶ help participants better appreciate the IF exploratory discussion process—especially its non-confrontational nature

- ▶ focus participants on the conceptual level

- ▶ help participants avoid advocating for a specific position

Step 5. Discussion of IF Report on Topic. The next step, and by far the longest part of your discussion, will involve a discussion of an IF Report. You start by asking the participants to compare their own concerns with those explored in the Report. You then move on to ask how the conceptual possibilities in the Report address their concerns and those described in the Report. Finally, you explore the consequences of the various conceptual possibilities. Allow the discussion to develop its own flow. Make sure that you avoid a forced march through the possibilities in the Report, and prevent the discussion from getting off topic.

After participants talk about their concerns regarding the topic at hand, redirect their attention to the Report. This means shifting gears, but not in the way you might think. This isn't a time for lengthy explanations of the possibilities, even if participants haven't read them before. Remember, this is a discussion, not a lecture or study group. The best way to get them all involved and focused on the Report right away is by having them read and then make a short comment on the Report's *summary* of conceptual possibilities, saving interactive discussion for later. Starting off with what we call a quick "lightening round"—getting a response from everyone to the full range of possibilities in the Report—is a great way to keep everyone involved as you refocus attention on the Report. This exercise is designed to elicit personal reaction to the possibilities. At the same time, be careful not to allow participants to get bogged down with fine-grained interpretation, criticism, or advocacy. This is another way the lightening round helps participants gain an appreciation for the full *range* of possibilities and get their exploratory feet wet. Finally, starting off this way gives the facilitator a good idea of which possibility is likeliest to make for a good starting point and also provides a "pre-discussion" picture of participants' thinking that can be compared to their thinking after the discussion series has been completed.

After gathering an initial reaction from everyone about the Report's set of possibilities as a whole, you're ready to begin considering them one by one. Again, be ready for non-linear discussion. Once you're into this more interactive stage, things may move slowly for a while, then suddenly leap forward, as various pieces of the discussion come together. The IF Report will help your discussion because it will let participants pitch their discussion at a conceptual level and keep them focused on the big picture rather than get mired in details. Discussing each possibility's possible consequences will highlight both its practicality and dependability on further choices about implementation.

Logically speaking, this is all a straightforward process: concerns (participants' then the Report's), possibilities, and then consequences. At times the actual discussion may feel messy, disjointed, and "all over the map." Even with a good facilitator, some of this is inevitable. Our thought processes and the discussion that's bound up with them are not "linear" but "organic"—they have a logic of their own, one that's interactive rather than one-dimensional. You may find yourself covering two or even more possibilities simultaneously, or part of two at one time. Your best guide in these situations is *to follow your participants' interests while keeping the overall content of the Report in mind*. It's their discussion, after all. Just do your best to keep it exploratory.

Throughout this process, the Report, perhaps illustrated by a large poster listing all of the possibilities that everyone can see—will be ready at hand, not to answer questions or provide an authoritative end point, but to supply additional contrasts. And because it is anonymous, the Report resists being treated like a political football.[1]

Step 6. Debriefing and Follow-Through. The final step in your discussion will be to talk over the experience with your group and ask participants to fill out a brief survey on it, preferably online. We'll describe these in depth in the next chapter.

FACILITATION

Listed at the end of this chapter, you'll find a list of IF publications chock-full of detailed facilitation tips and tricks. We heartily recommend that you make use of them. Here we're going to cover only the essentials.

Above all else, remember that to encourage the exploration of contrasts, the facilitator must be dynamic—not passive or mechanical. At the same time, remember that a facilitator is different from a participant. Your role is not that of a "player" but rather part referee, part coach. This means that your job involves much more than simply alternating speakers. Giving everyone a say can't by itself guarantee exploration.[2] To make room for the differing perspectives that mark real exploration, the facilitator must sometimes insist that participants play by the rules (as a referee would) and at other times encourage participants to stay focused on the "game" of generating, exploring, and developing alternatives (as a coach would).

The first step as referee/coach is to prepare a rulebook (or set of guidelines) and map out a game plan, which means familiarizing yourself with your participants and, even more important, with the report they'll be discussing (see Chapter 6). The more prepared you are the better you'll do come game time.

The next steps are to promote active listening, then constructive co-exploration. How? We've already discussed the first technique: guidelines by which the participants explicitly agree to be bound.

Don't be shy about reminding participants of this commitment. Remember the importance of being an assertive referee. The following table puts these in context and adds a few other facilitation do's and don'ts:

DON'T...	DO...
Let participants get sidetracked into debate or advocacy efforts to develop a consensus	Keep the focus on the exploration of contrasts:
	If it is, your discussion will be inclusive of a range of views
	If it isn't, ask participants what other concepts they can come up with or what concept other people might come up with
Let participants dwell on technical problem solving	Keep the discussion on the conceptual or general level by using prompts like:
	Can you generalize from that example?
	How can you tie that back to the topic we agreed to discuss?
Let participants get bogged down in arguments over the meaning of words[3]	Keep the focus on the content of concepts
	Encourage thinking beyond the usual meaning of words
Let a rigid schedule control the flow	Allow the discussion to be fluid
	Allow participants to pursue their own understandings of the possibilities and interests
Let pessimism or cynicism deflate your discussion	Recall examples of big historical change
	Contrast exploratory discussion with "canned" debates and pie-in-the-sky thinking
	Remind participants that no one can foresee the future

Table 7.1. Facilitation Do's and Don'ts for Exploratory Discussions

A NOTE ABOUT TAKING NOTES

Our research is clear on one final point: Notes aren't essential, and they should never keep you from performing your main tasks as coach and referee. But they are helpful if you plan to provide periodic summaries between meetings, which can ensure that everyone is on the same page and make participants feel appreciated. A concluding summary is a nice way to express your thanks and the sense that you value everyone's contribution. Feel free to experiment with technology as you document, share, and review discussion points. Notes can also be helpful in completing a brief debriefing of your experiences on Survey Monkey (see Chapter 8), which would be helpful to IF as we continue our efforts to improve both our process and our reports.

Visual representations of the discussion, on the other hand, are usually a good idea, since being able to see what has been said helps participants stay on task.

CONDUCTING AN IF PUBLIC DISCUSSION—A SINGLE RULE OF THUMB

While IF public discussions aren't "facilitator proof," they're close. At the beginning of this chapter we said that anyone who can maintain some order and spur people to try on new ways of thinking could hold a successful IF-style discussion. And while we've added some additional pointers here, keep those watchwords—*order* and *alternatives*—in mind. In fact, without order you're not going to have a discussion worthy of the name, so you could even boil that down to a single rule of thumb: As long as your group is exploring conceptual alternatives, it will be headed in the right direction—or, rather, direction*s*. And remember this: the challenges that come up during facilitation are part of learning the ropes. As you learn to handle various difficulties, you'll grow more skilled and confident and your discussions more robust and interesting.

A LIST OF RESOURCES

Website of the Interactivity Foundation: www.interactivity-foundation.org. Again, this resource is listed first because it is the single best way to access all of the materials you might want to consult as you plan this phase of the discussion.

Facilitation Guidebook for Small Group Public Discussions: Contains tips on all aspects of planning and conducting pubic discussions. Available at no cost in printed form directly from IF (order through IF Website, above, or mail request to P.O. Box 9; Parkersburg, West Virginia; 26102-0009). Also downloadable directly from the IF Website (see above).

Perspectives on Public Discussion: Background material in the form of postings from IF Fellows and collaborators on doing IF-style discussions. Downloadable directly from the IF Website (see above).

Public Discussion as the Exploration and Development of Contrasting Conceptual Possibilities. The most extensive analysis of IF's approach to public discussion. Available at no cost in printed form directly from IF (order through IF Website, above, or mail request to P.O. Box 9; Parkersburg, West Virginia; 26102-0009). Also downloadable directly from the IF Website (see above).

Contrasting Possibilities and the Interactivity Foundation Discussion Process. A relatively short but comprehensive introduction to the IF discussion process, with a special focus on the role of contrasts and commentary on how the IF process relates to current deliberative experiments in the People's Republic of China. Adolf G. Gundersen. 2005. Available at no cost in printed form directly from IF (order through IF Website, above, or mail request to P.O. Box 9; Parkersburg, West Virginia; 26102-0009). Also downloadable directly from the IF Website (see above).

"Just-In-Time Exploratory Public Discussion." Adolf G. Gundersen and Dennis Boyer. In *The Journal of Public Deliberation*, Volume 8 (2012), Issue 1. A case study in using current events to motivate participation in public discussions. Available at no cost in printed form directly from IF (order through IF Website, above, or mail request to P.O. Box 9; Parkersburg, West Virginia; 26102-0009). Also downloadable directly from the IF Website (see above).

Julius "Jay" Stern 1913-2009: A Biography. A lively and personal biography of IF founder Jay Stern. Natalie Hopkinson. 2010. Parkersburg, WV: Interactivity Foundation. Available at no cost in printed form directly from IF (order through IF Website, above, or mail request to P.O. Box 9; Parkersburg, West Virginia; 26102-0009). Also downloadable directly from the IF Website (see above).

NOTES

1. See Adolf G. Gundersen, *Public Discussion as the Exploration and Development of Contrasting Conceptual Possibilities*, published by the Interactivity Foundation, Parkersburg, West Virginia, November 2006: http://www.interactivityfoundation.org/resources-downloads/papers, (essay S-2, "Staff Work Reports for Public Discussion").

2. Ibid., essay U-5, "The Senses in Which Public Discussion is Democratic."

3. The reason for avoiding such arguments is that they hinder rather than promote further exploration:

   > Whether for psychological motives or because they are bent on advocating a particular policy, some citizens' desire to "win" will express itself as an attempt to exercise control over language. Other citizens will equate precision with clear thinking, forgetting

that the aim of exploration and developmental discussion is not precision, but the multiplication and clarification of possibilities. Still others, concerned above all with achieving some form of consensus, will forego true exploration and development as long as they are satisfied that those present are in agreement about how to express themselves.

By contrast, the general approach to language described here is one of maintaining a certain distance or caution about language: by guarding against the impulse to "get it right," by being aware of its obvious and potential limitations, and by remembering that while language may be an "end in itself" in other contexts, in public discussion it is not. Language should serve public discussion, rather than the reverse (ibid., essay A-6, "Language and Public Discussion").

4. Material in this section draws on Boyer, Dennis. "Practical Tips for Citizen Discussion of Possibilities: Part III- Managing and Wrapping Up A Discussion: Perspective on Interactivity:" http://www.interactivityfoundation.org, March 2, 2010.

CHAPTER 8

— *How to Follow Up an IF-Style Public Discussion*

To follow up an IF discussion, you'll want to do three things—besides thanking everyone for their participation, of course—the last of which is really a favor to IF:

- ▶ Debrief about the discussion experience itself

- ▶ If there's interest, plan another discussion

- ▶ Ask participants to complete IF's online survey[1]

Once the discussion is over, you should have a dialogue *about* the discussion. How did it feel? What did people find useful? What would they change? You might also find that there's interest in having another discussion. If so, strike while the iron is hot and make some initial arrangements to schedule a second (or third) discussion, and select a topic so that you have time to request materials from IF.[2] Finally, you'll want to ask participants to complete IF's short survey. The surveys are a key part of our ongoing research. Even more important, they contribute directly and critically to our quality improvement: the feedback we get from the survey helps us improve the way we do public discussions. All of this need take only about a half an hour, though you may find that participants enjoy it and want to hang around long after the "official" discussion is over to keep talking about the topic or about the discussion itself.

DEBRIEF

The main purpose of a debriefing session is to give everyone an opportunity to react to the overall discussion. This is valuable in itself because it further validates everyone's participation. It shows that their thinking about the discussion, not just their thinking during the discussion, matters. It's also a good time to revisit any complaints or concerns about the Report, the discussion process (or anything else!) that you might have deflected or deferred earlier so that the discussion could move forward.[3] But it can also be very revealing about what worked, what didn't, and why. There's no need to take notes on the discussion, though anything you record can prove useful as a reference when it comes time for the facilitator to fill out the feedback survey that we ask everyone to complete.

EXPLORE OTHER POSSIBLE "NEXT STEPS"

IF public discussions frequently end with participants energized and wanting to "do something more" than talk; they want to get involved in action. While engaging in direct advocacy would clearly be beyond IF's organizational mission, citizens are free to engage in the democratic process however they wish. More to the point, exploratory discussions of possibilities for citizen action—possible next steps—is both in keeping with the spirit of IF discussions and can give participants a greater feeling of closure at the same time.

ASK PARTICIPANTS TO FILL OUT IF'S SURVEY

We don't expect you to engage in any lengthy reporting about your experience with IF's public discussions. You may want to write it up for your group newsletter, a community bulletin, a blog, a local news outlet, or a press release (if you do, we'd love to hear about it!). But we do hope you will fill out our simple—and anonymous—online survey, which takes between 10 and 20 minutes, depending upon how much effort you put into it. There are separate versions for facilitators and participants; links to both can be found on the Foundation's Website (www. interactivityfoundation.org). Instructions for filling them out are located there, too.

Not all of your participants will have a computer or access to one. We'd still appreciate hearing from them. If you're willing to print out a paper copy of the survey, direct participants to send it to:

Interactivity Foundation

P.O. Box 9

Parkersburg, West Virginia 26102-0009

We'll make sure that their responses are recorded.

FOLLOWING UP ON THE DISCUSSION— A CHECKLIST

▶ Thank everyone for coming and contributing

▶ Debrief

▶ Plan another discussion, if there's interest

▶ Explore other possible "next steps"

▶ Ask participants to complete IF's online survey and explain how to access it through the Foundation's Website (www.interactivityfoundation.org)

NOTES

1. If you are especially energetic, you might also explore possibilities for building on the discussion between or after meetings, with or without interactive technology.

2. If there is interest in having another IF discussion, pass around a sign-up list. You might even plan more than one subsequent discussion, if there's a particular sequence of topics that makes sense to everyone. If you can put together enough repeaters for a discussion, great. Even lining up a few, however, makes organizing another discussion that much easier.

3. Thanks to IF Fellow Dennis Boyer for this insight.

APPENDIX I

— *IF Public Discussions in the Constellation of Democratic Discourse and Deliberation*

What is the place of IF public discussions within the larger constellation of democratic discourse and deliberation? This Appendix provides three answers to that question, each pitched at a different level of generality. The first and most general addresses the question from the standpoint of the American political process, the second by contrasting IF with 11 other well-known discussion models, and the third by comparing IF public discussions to a number of its closest "cousins."

IF PUBLIC DISCUSSIONS AND THE POLICY-MAKING PROCESS[1]

Let's start out with a textbook picture of how policy making works in the United States. It is a view of how the policy-making process really *does* work; it also conforms to a number of widely shared expectations about how it *should* work. These qualities make it useful as a starting point for thinking about how public discussion might relate to the practical world of actual policy making, and the sequence or order among the various steps or stages in the policy-making process, though apparently "fixed," actually helps highlight the essential contingency of the process, i.e. that citizens are free to consider where and how best to enter into it.

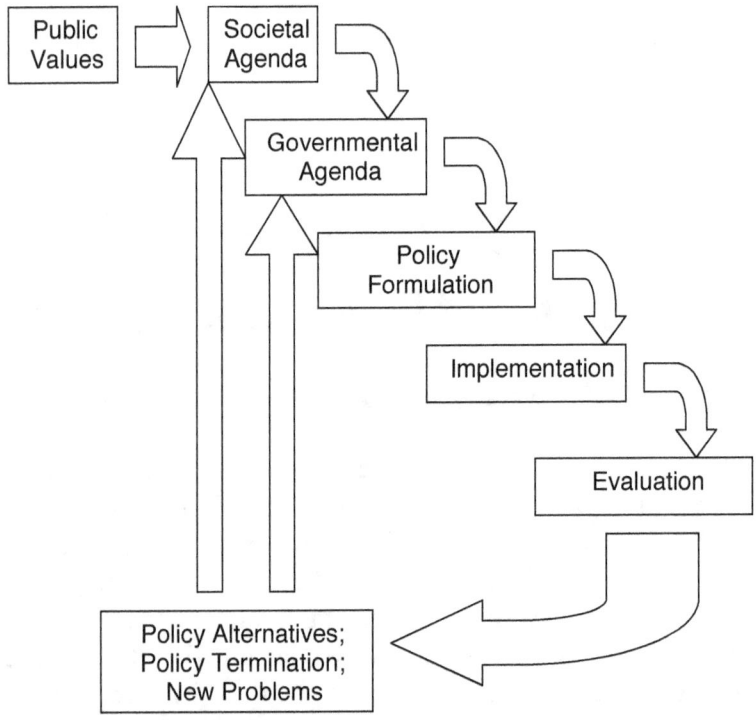

Figure AI.1 The Policy-Making Process (Adapted from American Government: Politics and Citizenship. Jerold L. Waltman. St. Paul: West Publishing, 1993. p. 390)

Figure A-1.1 may look comprehensive, but it is only a starting point. Indeed, it may well conceal more than it reveals.

Consider the following, all of which are absent from Figure AI.1:

- *Emotions, habits, beliefs, attitudes, assumptions, norms, concepts, and concerns.* (What the public cares about and how it cares about it are reduced to the cramped category of "public values.")

- A description of *how* "public values" are—or might be— formulated. ("Public values," held as the basic source of public policy, are taken as givens.)

- A description of how the "societal agenda" and the "government agenda" are *connected.* (The accompanying text identifies only three possibilities: interest groups, policy entrepreneurs, and political parties [Waltman 1993: 385].)

- A description of *how* "policy alternatives," "policy termination," and "new problems" *influence* "public values." (Although the text accompanying the chart indicates that such a connection exists, it merits no connecting arrow in the chart.)

In short, although political scientists are increasingly challenging the notion that citizens' largely unexamined and mostly individual "values" are—or should be—the proper and exclusive "source" of policy, that notion remains deeply entrenched, in and outside of academia. So, too, does the assumption that policy outcomes have little or no impact on "public values."

What might fill in these gaps? —two interactive concepts. The first would replace the concept of "public values" (top left of the Figure AI.1.) with a more expansive, inclusive, and practical description of citizens' orientations to the choices they in the present. The second concept would link this present-oriented description of what goes into citizens' immediate choices to a dynamic description of how citizens' arrive at choices. This dynamic description would bridge the gaps in the flow chart between "the public" and "societal agenda" and between policy outcomes (bottom right of Figure AI.1) and "the public" (upper left of Figure AI.1.). It would, in other words, describe how the public might be involved at the beginning of the policy-making process and how it might be affected by the results of the policy-making process.

"Democratic discussion" is such a concept. It is a shorthand way of referring to various processes that involve citizens in policy making through the medium of discussion. IF-style public discussion is one kind of democratic discussion among others—although of a very distinctive sort. IF public discussions are democratic discussions in which citizens interactively explore and develop selected areas of concern (among which will figure the results of past policy making), contrasting possibilities for addressing them, and test the consequences of applying these possibilities. As is explained in greater detail below, this means that public discussion is particularly well suited to contexts in which policy making has not yet reached the stage of actual decision making or action.

Most believers in democratic discussion focus their attention on one or another stage of policy making. The broadest division is between those who think that democratic discussion's most important contribution is to the "societal agenda" (or to what is sometimes called "preference formation") and those who believe that democratic discussion should be used at the point of "policy formulation" (or "will formation"). IF's style of public discussions are aimed primarily at the former: toward the discussion of public policy *before* decisions or actual choices are on the table (though it begins with an area of concern rather than "preferences" and concludes with contrasting conceptual possibilities rather than an "agenda").

The view that public discussion—whether based on prior public discussion or a sanctuary staff work report—might best be used in this way results from two closely interactive considerations: the first related to current limitations of citizen policy

Let's Talk Politics

discussion, the second related to where—or when—public discussion can be most useful. Both point in the same direction.

Many of the limitations of current democratic discussion that can be addressed by public discussion[2] are clearly best addressed *early* in the policy-making process, including:

▶ Broad conceptual exploration and development of areas of concern

▶ Broad conceptual exploration and development of possibilities

▶ Broad exploration and development of possible practical consequences through testing.

All of these require the kind of deliberate, reflective, pace that only time (and patience) allow. The closer the point at which policy is enacted, the less time is available to address them and the more advocacy is likely to intrude on the discussion.

Democratic discussion is most likely to have a positive impact on both citizens' thinking and policy choices (whether exercised directly or through representatives) when conducted before the actual stage of policy formulation and decision.

▶ The closer the discussion is in time to actual decisions, the more it will tend to be subject to manipulation, "influence," and advocacy for particular interests or results.

▶ The prospect of even relatively proximate decisions may lead citizens to think that further discussion is unnecessary.

▶ Actual decisions may effectively put at least a temporary stop to discussion.

IF PUBLIC DISCUSSIONS AND THE OTHER BASIC TYPES OF DISCUSSION, DIALOGUE, DISCOURSE, AND DELIBERATION

"Discussion," "discourse," "dialogue," and "deliberation" may all sound like the same thing, and on some very general level, that is true. But there is huge variety among them (and their variants) in practice, based on purpose, process, and product: so much variety, in fact, that there are now numerous catalogues or typologies that have been created to make sense of them all.[3] Let's start with one of the simplest, published by an umbrella group called the National Coalition for Dialogue and Deliberation (NCDD), made up of scholars, practitioners, and activists. Called "Streams of Practice," NCDD's discussions are divided into four basic types: decision making, collaborative action, exploration, and conflict transformation.[4] IF's public discussions involve neither decision making nor collaborative action; they're not intended to yield outcomes of this sort. (Nor are they intended to produce peace where before there was strife; this is what mediation strives for.[5]) Instead, they are characterized by what two well-known scholars have called "low-decision control."[6] What they are intended to do is engage participants in exploration, which in turn is expected to promote civility, which qualifies as a certain kind of "conflict transformation." So IF's public discussions clearly straddle two of NCDD's four basic categories.

IF PUBLIC DISCUSSIONS CONTRASTED WITH 11 OTHER SPECIFIC FORMS OF DISCUSSION[7]

Let's narrow the focus now down further. Civic discourse is often thought of and practiced as advocacy or debate, sometimes as a calm or disinterested exchange of reasons, and on other occasions, as a hybrids of these with elements from mediation and other processes. IF's public discussions involve something different: an interactive process of exploring, developing, and testing contrasting conceptual possibilities for democratic governance in selected areas of concern.

Most other discussion models are, like the IF process, complex in their own ways. For that reason, comparing them is like comparing one fruit salad to another. To use the metaphor with which this chapter began, you might say that discursive forms exist in a constellation, arrayed not as black and white or even as points in a spectrum, but as wholly different sorts of bodies in space. Still, some comparisons will help you see what is distinctive about IF discussions and where they overlap with other forms of discourse.

In this section we try to bring the distinctiveness of IF public discussions into sharper focus by comparing them with 11 familiar forms of democratic discussion. Table AI.1 on pages 116-117 describes these other forms. Each row of the table represents a different form of democratic discussion. (The rows are divided into two broad categories: those, like IF public discussion, that are intended to inform, educate, or broaden the public's policy thinking and those that, alternatively, are intended to yield some form of decision or action, whether it be problem-solving consensus, compromise, recommendations, problem solving, or actual decisions[7]) Table AI.1's column headings indicate four key aspects of IF public discussion. Check marks indicate where the other forms of democratic discussion chosen for comparison appear to incorporate a particular aspect of IF public discussion; X's indicate where they do not appear to do so. And question marks indicate where no clear judgment appears possible either way. Below each mark are bullets for clarification.

Table AI.1. Contrasts between IF Public Discussion and Eleven Selected Forms of Democratic Discussion

| Form of Discussion | Key Aspects of Public Discussion of IF Citizens Staff Work Reports | | | |
	Interactivity	Exploration & Development of Conceptual Possibilities	Small Groups of Citizens	Trained Facilitators
Form of Discussion				
Aimed at Decision Making or Action				
Parliamentary Bodies	X • decision making • advocacy	X • decisions • procedures, rules	X • usually > 20 members • elected	X • trained in rules • highly directive
Town Hall Meetings	? • may or may not be collaborative	X • decisions • procedures, rules	X • usually > 20 persons	?
Direct Democracy (Small Groups)	? • may or may not be collaborative	X • decisions (often by consensus)	?	?
"Bureaucratic Networks" (see note at bottom of Table)	? • may or may not be collaborative	? • most often problem-solving • often technical	X • officials	?
Expert Commissions	? • may or may not be collaborative	X • decisions (positive recommendations) • often technical	X • experts, authorities, specialists	X • trained in producing answers
Supreme Court Deliberations	? • may or may not be collaborative	X • decisions (rulings of law) • formal legal rules	X • legal specialists	? • trained in legal processes
Juries	✓	X • decisions (verdicts) • facts	X • representative, neutral	? • may lack training

Table A1.1. (continued) Contrasts between IF Public Discussion and Selected Forms of Democratic Discussion

	Key Aspects of Public Discussion of IF Citizens Staff Work Reports			
	Interactivity	Exploration & Development of Conceptual Possibilities	Small Groups of Citizens	Trained Facilitators
Form of Democratic Discussion				
Aimed at Informing, Educating, or Broadening the Public's Policy Thinking				
Public Hearings	X • citizens do not interact • public officials may ignore citizens	X • plans • advocacy • formal rules	X • many participants	? • trained in procedure
Debate	X • advocacy, not collaborative	X • advocacy of "given" positions • formal rules	X • two sides • often are "experts"	? • trained in managing debate
Mass Media	X • mostly one-way flow from "source" to "user"	X • information, persuasion, entertainment	X • individual readers, viewers • often "experts"	? • trained in "objectivity," debate, entertainment
Issues Forums	X • series of set speeches rather than discussion	X • citizens react to pre-established "positions" • formal rules	X • many participants	? • trained in enforcing rules

* Bureaucratic networks result from and sustain informal and formal discursive interactions among government officials, usually in the executive branch of government. The degree to which they are "democratic" probably varies a great deal, but much the same could be said of each of the alternative types of democratic discussion listed here.

CONTRASTS BETWEEN IF PUBLIC DISCUSSIONS AND OTHER FAMILIAR FORMS OF PUBLIC DISCUSSION

Reading across the table's *rows* in Table AI.1 reveals three broad patterns:

▶ No other form of democratic discussion embodies all four key aspects of IF's public discussion.

▶ All of the alternative forms of democratic discussion aimed at informing, educating, or broadening the public's policy thinking (those on the second page of the table) lack at least three of the four key aspects of IF public discussion.

▶ Jury deliberations are perhaps most like IF public discussion. Nevertheless, there remain two crucial differences between the two processes: Juries properly (1) focus on "the facts" (rather than possibilities, conceptual possibilities at that); and (2) are charged with making decisions—"rendering a verdict" (rather than exploring and developing an area of concern and conceptual possibilities for addressing it). In all other cases, the differences between alternative forms of democratic discussion and IF public discussion are both as significant and more numerous.

Reading down the table's four *columns* helps clarify further the contrasts between IF public discussion and other forms of democratic discussion by drawing attention to the particular aspects of IF public discussion that are most often lacking in other forms of democratic discussion. Reading the table down each column shows that:

▶ While interactivity can characterize other forms of democratic discussion, it usually happens "by accident" rather than through reliance on regular supports such as specially crafted discussion reports, a well-developed exploratory process, active facilitation and/or small groups. The two exceptions are the Supreme Court and jury deliberations—both of which significantly diverge from IF public discussion in being aimed at (legal) decisions rather than conceptual exploration and development of contrasting conceptual possibilities.

▶ None of the other 11 forms of democratic discussion regularly engage in the exploration and development of conceptual possibilities. "Bureaucratic networks" perhaps do so occasionally, but only by resisting the need—ever present in bureaucracies—to solve the immediate practical problems of government.

▶ Juries probably come closest to relying on small groups of diverse citizens. With 12 members, the typical jury perhaps qualifies as a small group of citizens. Yet the two processes most often used to constitute juries (random selection and *voir dire*) are intended to promote representativeness and neutrality rather than diverse views—and may even have the effect of discouraging them. Though important in courtroom settings, both representativeness and neutrality can discourage the kind of unorthodox or unconventional thinking most useful in the exploratory and developmental discussion of conceptual possibilities.

Most of the other forms of democratic discussion have a question mark in the facilitator column because while they typically rely on facilitators, facilitators may be focused on *different purposes* from those that motivate IF discussions. (Those marked "X" are so marked not because they lack trained facilitators, but rather because the facilitator is there to do something other than encourage exploratory and developmental discussion; indeed, they are often very good at hindering it or squelching it altogether.)

Table AI.1. represents only a sample of the variety of discussion processes in use today. An increasing number of scholars and citizens' groups have been promoting various forms of democratic discussion over the past three decades.[8] Their motives vary, and they tend to disagree over the questions of where and how to insert democratic discussion into the policy-making process. At the end of the day, however, it is probably best to pay these quarrels only so much heed. Just as there is no single form of democratic discussion, there is no single point at which democratic discussion should be inserted into the policy-making process. Democratic discussion can take multiple useful forms; democratic discussion can be made part of nearly any stage of policy making (even "implementation"). And, as we've tried to show throughout this short book, democratic discussion can make a powerful contribution to civility as well.

NOTES

1. This section borrows from material previously published as "Democratic Discussion, Public Discussion, and the Policy-Making Process," Essay U-1 and "Some Limitations of Current Democratic Discussion," Essay U-2 in Adolf G. Gundersen, *Public Discussion as the Exploration and Development of Contrasting Conceptual Possibilities.* Report published by the Interactivity Foundation, Parkersburg, West Virginia, November 2006: http://www.interactivityfoundation.org/resources-downloads/papers, pp. 79-84, 85-100.

2. For an extended discussion of current limitations on public discourse—and how IF public discussions address them— see Essay U-2 in Adolf G. Gundersen, *Public Discussion as the Exploration and Development of Contrasting Conceptual Possibilities.* Report published by the Interactivity Foundation, Parkersburg, West Virginia, November 2006: http://www.interactivityfoundation.org/resources-downloads/papers, pp. 79-84, 85-100.

3. See, for example, Figure 3.1 on p. 59 of Adolf G. Gundersen's *The Socratic Citizen* (Lanham, Md.: Lexington Books, 2000), which focuses on the number of participants. The National Coalition for Dialogue and Deliberation online document "Engagement Streams Framework." available at http://www.ncdd.org/files/NCDD2010_Engagement_Streams.pdf, contains a more applied typology, cross-referenced by various criteria, and lists several additional typologies.

4. Again, see http://www.ncdd.org/files/NCDD2010_Engagement_Streams.pdf.

5. The term "mediation" refers to an entire family of processes all aimed at arriving at negotiated agreements, usually as a way of avoiding arbitration (an externally imposed settlement), litigation, or continuing conflict. Mediation's goal is to replace war with peace, without the armed conflict. It may lead in the longer run to civility, but mediation's immediate goal is simply a cessation of hostilities. In this it is very different from discussion processes that have participants explore alternatives in order to learn or engage in dialogue to improve the way they relate to each other. Mediation also usually involves a facilitator with special authority and particular procedural rules—both of which are either less pronounced or wholly absent in the case of exploratory discussion and transformative dialogue. Mediation, in short, is distinct both in terms of the formality of its process and in terms of how decisive (and binding) are its results.

6. See Christopher F. Karpowitz and Jane Mansbridge, "Disagreement and Consensus: The Importance of Dynamic Updating in Public Deliberation," in *The Deliberative Democracy Handbook,* ed. John Gastil and Peter Levine (San Francisco: Jossey-Bass, 2005), 244.

7. This section draws upon material originally published as "Interactivity Foundation Public Discussion Contrasted with Other Forms of Democratic Discussion," Essay IF-3 and "The Distinctiveness of Public Discussion," Essay U-4 in Adolf G. Gundersen, *Public Discussion as the Exploration and Development of Contrasting Conceptual Possibilities*. Report published by the Interactivity Foundation, Parkersburg, West Virginia, November 2006: http://www.interactivityfoundation.org/resources-downloads/papers, pp. 11-15, pp. 107-09.

8. For a recent collection of theoretical perspectives on democratic deliberation, see *Democratizing Deliberation: An Anthology*. 2012. Barker, Derek W.M., Noëlle McAfee, and David W. McIvor, Eds. Dayton, Ohio: Kettering Foundation Press. Those curious about the practice of democratic deliberation should start by having a look at the homepage of the National Coalition for Dialogue and Deliberation: http://www.ncdd.org.

APPENDIX II

— Participant Demographics

The charts and graphs that follow summarize the demographic composition of IF's first several hundred participants. As IF broadens its participant base (a practical imperative given the democratic nature of IF's mission), we should see more variation within the demographic make-up of our participants. Note that these demographic summaries represent only the 700 participants (about 40-50% of our total number of discussion participants) who filled out an IF survey at the end of their discussions.

Sex?

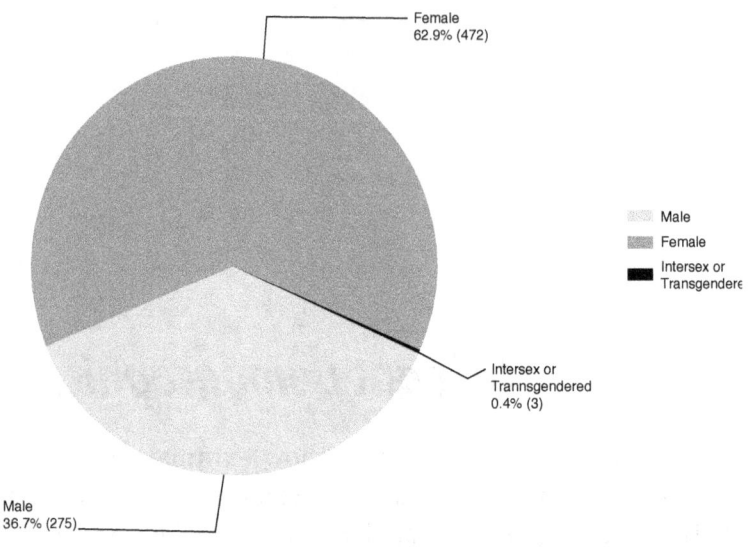

Figure AII.1. Sex of IF Public Discussion Participants

Nationally, according to the 2011 *American Community Survey[1]*, the U.S. population comprises 50.8% women. It is estimated that .25-1% of the U.S. population is transgendered and about 1.7% is intersex.[2]

Let's Talk Politics

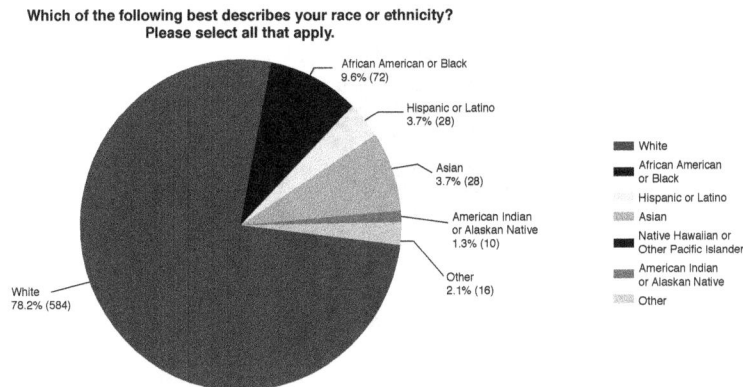

Figure AII.2. Race and/or Ethnicity of IF Public Discussion Participants

According to the 2011 *American Community Survey*, 78.1% of the U.S. population is white (63.4% are white persons, non-Hispanic), 13.1% is African American or black, 16.7% is Hispanic or Latino, 5% is Asian, .2% is Native Hawaiian or other Pacific Islander, and 1.2% is American Indian or Alaskan Native.

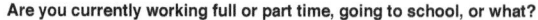

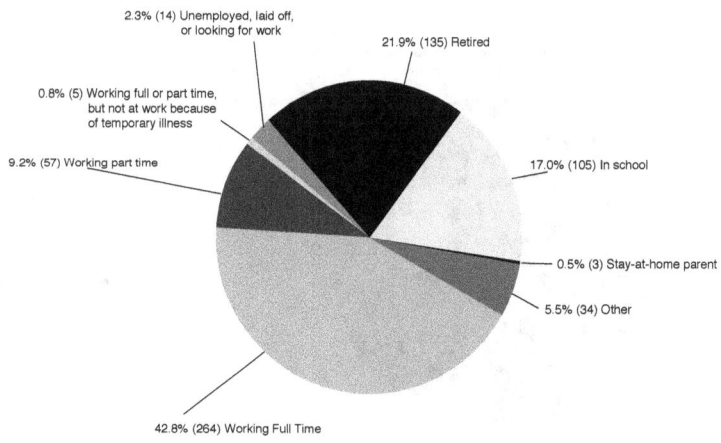

2.3% (14) Unemployed, laid off, or looking for work

21.9% (135) Retired

0.8% (5) Working full or part time, but not at work because of temporary illness

9.2% (57) Working part time

17.0% (105) In school

0.5% (3) Stay-at-home parent

5.5% (34) Other

42.8% (264) Working Full Time

Figure AII.3. Occupation of IF Public Discussion Participants

According to Gallup.com, the percentage of Americans (age 16 and older) who are working full time is approximately 47%. Another 11.3% are working part time. As of November 2012, 7.7% were unemployed (Current Population Survey [http://www.bls.gov/cps/]). Approximately 1.2% are off work due to a temporary illness, or for some other reason (Current Population Survey). According to the Bureau of Labor Statistics, approximately 6.7% of Americans are in school full time and about another 12.2% are retired; as many as 10.9% are self-employed, and about .37% are stay-at-home moms or dads. (Note: Total percentages may not add up to 100% due to rounding.)

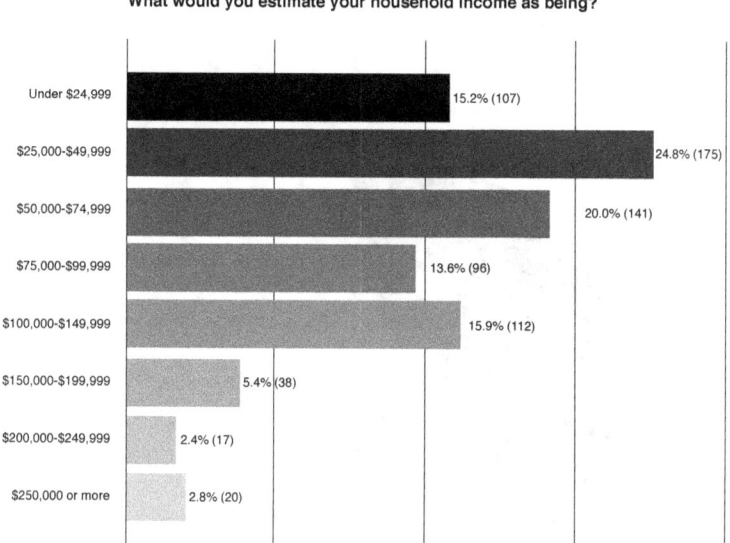

What would you estimate your household income as being?

Income	Percent (count)
Under $24,999	15.2% (107)
$25,000-$49,999	24.8% (175)
$50,000-$74,999	20.0% (141)
$75,000-$99,999	13.6% (96)
$100,000-$149,999	15.9% (112)
$150,000-$199,999	5.4% (38)
$200,000-$249,999	2.4% (17)
$250,000 or more	2.8% (20)

Figure AII.4. Income of IF Public Discussion Participants

Median income among our respondents was $62,498. Median household income in the United States for 2011 was $50,054 (U.S. Census Bureau).[3]

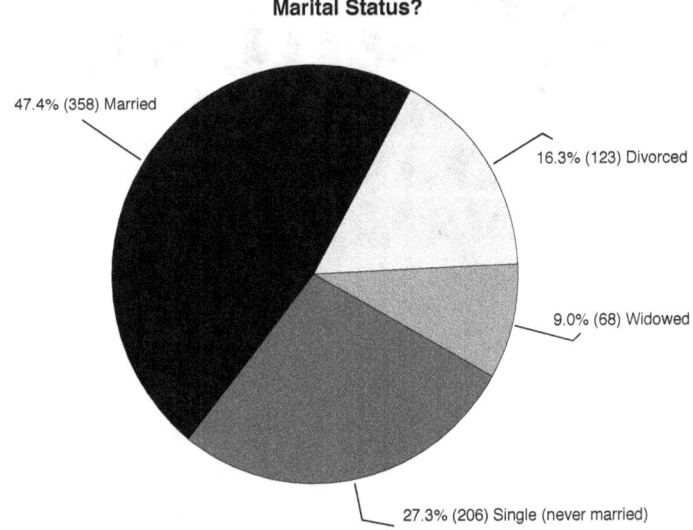

Figure AII.5. Marital Status of IF Public Discussion Participants

According to the 2011 *American Community Survey,* 48.3% of Americans are married, 6% are widowed, 11% are divorced, and 32.5% have never been married.

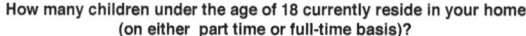

How many children under the age of 18 currently reside in your home (on either part time or full-time basis)?

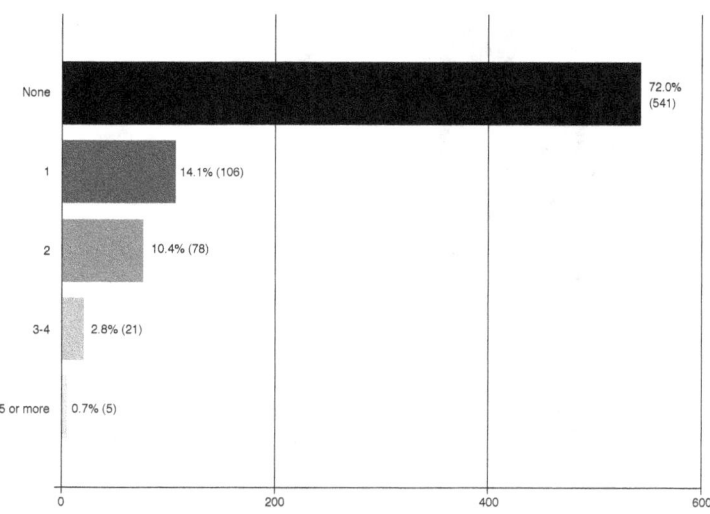

Figure AII.6. Number of Children of IF Public Discussion Participants

In 2009, the number of U.S. households in which children under the age of 18 resided reached its lowest point in half a century: just 46%. Clearly, however, the average participant in an IF discussion is even less likley to have children living at home, because she or he is either retired, possibly has grown children who have left home, or is a younger person who has never had children.[4]

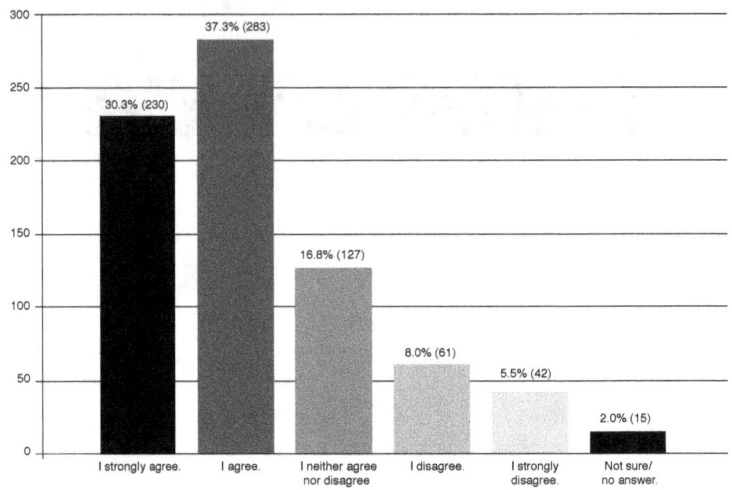

Government should do more to address society's problems. Would you say that you agree or disagree with this statement?

Figure AII.7. Attitude Towards Government Involvement in Economic and Social Issues of IF Public Discussion Participants

A 2010 Gallup Governance Survey found 22% of Americans prefer less government involvement in social and economic issues, and 20% prefer more active government in social and economic issues.[5]

NOTES

1. The *American Community Survey* is a statistical survey that samples a small percentage of U.S. households each year. It is conducted by the U.S. Census Bureau.

2. See the Intersex Society of North America (http://www. isna.org/faq/frequency) and National Center for Transgendered Equality (http://transequality.org/Resources/ NCTE_UnderstandingTrans.pdf) for more details about these statistics.

3. This statistic is explored in "U.S. Income Gap Rose, Sign of Uneven Recovery," by Sabrina Tavernise in *The New York Times* (September 12, 2012). Web link: http://www. nytimes.com/2012/09/13/us/us-incomes-dropped-last-year-census-bureau-says.html?_r=0

4. This statistic is discussed in "Number of Households with Kids Hits New Low," by Jack Gillum of *USA Today* (February 26, 2009). Web link: http://usatoday30.usatoday.com/ news/nation/census/2009-02-25-families-kids-home_N. htm.

5. See http://www.gallup.com/poll/143624/majorities-view-gov-intrusive-powerful.aspx (Lydia Saad, *GALLUP Politics*, October 13, 2010).

About the Authors

Adolf G. Gundersen

Adolf G. Gundersen's work as Fellow and Research Director of the Interactivity Foundation has added a new, practical dimension to a career devoted to understanding and promoting public discussion as a teacher, theorist, policy analyst, and social scientist.

Gundersen's academic publications include three books, two of which deal specifically with public discussion (The Environmental Promise of Democratic Deliberation, University of Wisconsin Press, 1995; and The Socratic Citizen, Lexington Books, 2000). His most recent publication, co-authored with colleague Dennis Boyer for The Journal of Public Deliberation, is titled "Just-in-Time Exploratory Public Discussion." Gundersen is also a past contributor to The Washington Post and CNN online.

Suzanne Goodney Lea

Suzanne Goodney Lea is a Fellow of the Interactivity Foundation. Previously, she served as an Associate Professor at Gallaudet University's Sociology Department and as Chair of the Criminal Justice Program at Trinity College, both in Washington, D.C.

Lea is an expert on race, gender, and the social construction of crime and criminal justice policy. She has provided analysis on these topics for ABC World News, The Guardian Unlimited, the BBC, NPR, and several local affiliates. Her current work explores group-based discourse in contemporary university classrooms and in public discussions, both here and in Asia. Additionally, she is working on a project exploring race and culture as it relates to university school shootings. Lea teaches a Policy Wars class for the Washington Center in D.C. and occasionally lectures on women, gender, and film at Towson University.